Copyright Annie Davison 2021

All rights reserved

The moral right of the author has been asserted

www.guidelines.uk.com

Annie Davison is a former national journalist and later an editorial consultant for WHO in Geneva. But over the last twenty five years, she has worked with individual clients through channelled guidance and held dozens of workshops and courses in the UK and France. Her wish has been to open the door to understanding that life is so much bigger than we could ever imagine.

She sees channelling as just the latest outcome of the long road to consciousness: witness to the vast arena and creativity of what it is to be fully human. A challenging journey but, she says, "to me it's the only journey worth taking".

Her books mirror her own spiritual journey: from *The Wise Virgin*, published in 1979, to this, her latest and ninth book and second memoir: '*A Place to Call home?*'

PRAISE FOR OTHER BOOKS BY ANNIE DAVISON

Under the name Annie Wilson:

The Wise Virgin (1979)

"A real inspiration to me. Thank you for the wisdom and beauty you led me to."

What Colour Are You? (with Lilla Bek: 1981 and 1987)

"Simply superb. A great supporting text for those studying the energy healing field."

As Annie Davison:

Time to Change: a guide to life after greed (2011)

"I pick up this book nearly every day and it gives me inspiration and nourishment every time.

Shadowplay: a novel (2016)

"The tension built up so brilliantly and flowed with great ease. It felt filmic in its scope with hints of The Magus by John Fowles."

A Spot to Stand: a memoir (2017)

"To be as conscious, deeply and vastly so, of your own journey and to 'know thyself' in this way, is a remarkable gift."

A PLACE TO CALL HOME?

Annie Davison

Teaching My Truth

"The greatest revolution of our generation is the discovery that human beings, by changing the inner attitudes of their minds, can change the outer aspects of their lives."
William James

"Imagination is more important than knowledge. For knowledge is limited whereas imagination embraces the entire world, stimulating progress, giving birth to evolution."
Albert Einstein

CHAPTER ONE

1995-1996: Daisy Bank

'Go home and start channelling'

In the early 1990s Kirsten Bolwig was my 'healer of choice'. I first met her in Bath, where I lived briefly after I left my home in Provence. I was drawn to her talk on the Bach Flower Remedies, and from there I decided to ask her for aromatherapy sessions. She worked from her home in Widcombe

In my memoir '*A Spot to Stand*', I explore the tumultuous years 1970-1995, and the journey towards consciousness. By which I mean, the awareness of each of us as a 'divine being', on a journey of integration, life after life, towards a spiritual understanding of ourselves to be part of a vast multi-dimensional existence with access to 'the universal mind'.

Once you 'answer the call', there is no turning back. And it is a tough call! In a life 'more bizarre than I would wish for yourself', as one astrologer described it, I had worked for twenty five years on 'clearing the clutter' of old personal and collective history, alongside an increasing sense of 'knowing' - exploring the art of healing, writing, and meeting the most extraordinary people along the way. For me, those years were punctuated with karmic relationships which were 'heaven and hell' simultaneously and took me on a roller coaster journey to 'know myself'.

But in 1989 I knew a moment of completion. The marker point was my last seminar with Ruth White – on Alchemy - at Le

Plan, the beautiful Provençal estate of Lorna St Aubyn. Le Plan was very close to my home in Le Castellet, where I had settled after my relationship with Austin in Geneva broke up.

I knew then I had done enough. From then on, the 'existential pain' of the spiritual journey would never be as bad again. But still, in 1992, Kirsten did an amazing job of loosening the lingering bits of battered psyche and helping me to embody fully all the experiences I had had over those brutal years. In 1994, on the completion of our work together, she just said it. "Go home and start channelling"! So, I did.

I was now living in Daisy Bank, a small cottage in a terrace that faced a large park in Stroud. I had finally sold my house in Le Castellet and could buy my first home back in England. It was thanks to Carole Bruce, who I had met at a seminar in Le Plan, that I came to Stroud and it was through her kindness that the landing was fairly gentle. Stroud was a hive of alternative thinking, and she introduced me to many like-minded friends.

Every day for two months and more I practised 'automatic writing'. I covered notebook after notebook with my attempts to 'hear' what was coming through to me. During the whole of 1994 Carole and I would spend hours together practising our art. She too was exploring the idea of channelling.

What I knew I wanted now, was to help people who were struggling on the same path, encountering the same psychic and spiritual dramas; facing the same darkness I had faced over the last twenty-five years, particularly in the last ten when I was living in the depths of the 'dark feminine' (portrayed in metaphor in my novel '*Shadowplay*'.)

I remembered a time in the early nineties - when walking through Regents Park, London, after an astrology workshop - I found myself in abject despair. When I reached the end of the park, a noticeboard outside St Pancras church offered a day of healing.

At that moment I knew nobody could help me; not even the very best teachers I had met along the way. This was my journey and I had to trust I would see it through. But I knew, too, that if ever I got out of that dark place, I would make it my business to help others out of it too.

Many years before, in the mid-eighties, when I attended the College of Healing in Malvern, the principal Herthe Larive had told me I was not a healer but a spiritual teacher. And I now felt it was my job to teach everything I knew.

In my first book, *'The Wise Virgin',* written in 1977, I had used the authority of such people as Carl Jung, Roberto Assagioli, Abraham Maslow, Michel Polyani, to explain my own experience. Now I wanted to express life through my own authority and to encourage others towards their own authenticity.

I was still doing automatic writing when I somehow found the courage to ask Irene Morley, who worked as a secretary at the College of Psychic Studies in London, if they needed another medium. I had met Irene at Le Plan. And in January 1995, I had a one-day-a-week job! Every Friday I would park my car in Cirencester and take the National Express to London.

I do not like the word 'Medium'. The original ethos of the College was 'proof of life after death'. As far as I knew the mediums would contact loved ones and give comfort and reassurance. But my own sense of things was that although the spiritual journey was necessarily psychic, the psychic was not necessarily spiritual.

The word channel is a confusing one. It refers in one word to a vast spectrum of experience and the problem, perhaps, is people opening up more and more to the astral levels of consciousness. To me, the astral or psychic gaze was old form, not new humanity and it was vital to distinguish the two. I saw the psychic as a material phenomenon, not a spiritual one, and I feel this is where mediumship belongs.

The new is concerned with the integrity of 'soul consciousness', rather than the glamour of psychic awareness. From my experience, the psychic ability to 'just come out with things' about another person is often about power and control and above all feeling 'special'.

I remember early on, in 1978, Lilla Bek warning against the dangers of uncontrolled psychism, when 'anything – good or bad' could come in. In my view, unless you have worked on the psychological issues you face, then your access to information will be tainted. Choosing a therapist who has 'done the work' is, for me, absolutely vital.

To me, it is important never to tune in about someone unless you are asked to do so; and never invade another person's privacy without their permission. The journey is about spiritual unfolding, not an attempt to harness clever psychic abilities. One client, who was incredibly psychic, comes to mind.

Our first work together was to close her down, in order to open up in a safer and more truthful way. The guides would make her aware that there is a difference: the experience not of feeling 'smug' about her gifts, but the neutrality of it being 'ordinary'. In that regard the College, whose early President was Sir Arthur Conan Doyle, had a salutary story.

In earlier days, two senior members made an agreement that when one of them passed over, they would get a message through to the other. When this happened the message, via a psychic said: "I'm just not as evolved as I thought I was!"

I wore a badge which said 'Medium', but I had to make it clear that I did not do mediumship. The girls on the desk would assign clients accordingly. In fact, the new head of the college who engaged me, was keen to bring the college more into 'the Light', the spiritual, and we spoke of those differences.

A case in point was a woman who had been to a spiritualist church and was told by the resident psychic that he saw a 'woman in red', sitting beside her. He said this woman would be her spirit guide. But when we worked together the client was able to see that the 'woman in the red dress' was part of her own psyche which was now ready to be integrated into her own sense of herself. Experiencing the effect of this was a revelation.

Another time a young man had come to consult a medium because he felt he was surrounded by aliens. Apart from the extraordinary fact of 'seeing' them, they were also telling him he would be a healer. He said that on one occasion he had been walking in woods with his sister and friends and they had experienced these aliens too.

My way of working is to take the client on a guided meditational journey. It is an immediate, experiential process, which enables clients to see and feel exactly what the wounds have been in this lifetime, possibly over many lifetimes. The guides would get straight to the heart of a matter, allowing the clients to experience for themselves the 'fact' of their experience, and the resolution.

It is not like a self-help book instilling change from the outside, but consciously changing your own unwanted patterns by experiencing their truth and moving through them. All done in dialogue with the guides.

The problem is never what you think it is, but always recognisable when you see it. I was totally present, detached, and able to perceive what was happening for the client. It turned out that what this man perceived as 'aliens' were parts of his own psyche that had split off – left the body – when he had been sexually assaulted by family as a child. We brought these aspects back into his body, showed him that indeed he would be a healer, but a safe one, embodied.

If he had worked from his alien standpoint, his healing would have been tainted with those unredeemed issues. It is by addressing the problems and coming to terms with them within ourselves and, importantly within the body, that the healing process enables us to begin living life to the full once again, with clarity of vision.

In fact, this client continued to do work with me after I had left the College, and his sister joined a healing course I did a few years later. His girlfriend, who was self-harming, also came to see me at the college and had occasional sessions with me for several years after. I was honoured to be invited to their wedding.

At this point I would say that many people who think they have been sexually assaulted, in fact have not been. During the writing of '*The Wise Virgin*', renowned astrologer and Jungian analyst, Liz Greene, had told me that often it is the unconscious desires of someone that affects the child, and this registers in the depths of the psyche as actual assault. In working with clients who brought this problem I also found this to be true.

After several years of working together, one client (and a regular workshop participant) finally had the courage to ask if her late husband really had sexually assaulted their two nieces, as claimed. He had always denied it, but this accusation had caused a rift in her family for many years. During the session she was able to perceive and understand that he had not physically touched the girls, but his unconscious had influenced their psyches and produced this 'false memory'.

One of my favourite clients was Phyllis. She had been consulting the mediums at the College for many years and I must have seen her about six times in the year I was there. Phyllis was

96 and had a sister of 105. Apparently, they frequently talked about these matters together, and Phyllis was always telling me how much she looked forward to passing over so she could satisfy her curiosity about it all.

It is important to say that this work is not 'fortune telling'. She knew I did not do 'proof of life', but one of her first missions was to ask me for the week's lottery numbers. She wanted enough money to help a young healer friend to set up a clinic! I had to tell her I could not do that either. And that if I could, I might have done it for myself long ago!

She often asked me to find things she had lost in her garden. And to tell her what to expect after death: what was the 'light at the end of the tunnel' like? What was the name of my guide so she could contact him when she passed over? She seemed happy with the things the guides were able to tell her.

I also saw occasional clients in Daisy Bank. I was still writing everything down, which must have made each session rather slow going. I also recorded the session on a cassette tape, to give to the client.

One client, a doctor, came because in two weeks she was to have an anal operation, with serious consequences. Through guidance she was shown – and relived - how at the age of four she had '*poo'd*' in her cot, just as her father had come through the door. She saw how the 'shame' of this incident, deeply buried in her subconscious and totally forgotten, had created 'anal issues' throughout her life, particularly affecting relationships. By seeing this incident and moving through, she no longer needed the operation.

Miracles like that are few. Though I like to think I had two babies! One client asked for help because she had difficulty conceiving. We discovered an incident in childhood where, in huge frustration, her mother had shut her in a cupboard. This imprisonment had unconsciously affected her relationship to motherhood. She conceived within two weeks.

Another client came because of constant miscarriages. She saw – and re-experienced - that in babyhood her own mother had clung on to her for dear life, for emotional support, and had almost 'strangled' her, literally and metaphorically. This affected my client in so many ways, including in her posture, particularly her neck. She, too, conceived soon after the session.

But mostly the uncovering of the vicissitudes of the human condition is a much slower and less dramatic experience, although unlike other therapies I did not, as a rule, need to see people regularly. Most people liked a top-up now and again, but the effect of a session could last for a long time and produce enough 'homework' for those who ran with the ball, for several months ahead. Sometimes the 'ah ha' could come a long time later.

Something I learned early on, was from a client who came to me with breast cancer, but who was determined not to take the allopathic path. We worked in the capacity of guidance on the inner blocks and barriers, but the symptoms got worse. I know, had I been her, I would have had a mastectomy, as advised by her consultant. My own sense of complementary therapy is it is just that, complementary. In most things of a serious nature I would always favour the medical route.

My client later died. I knew she had made her own choices and I knew I was not the only practitioner she was consulting. But I wished I had made it clear each time - as I do now when people bring me medical issues - that I do not claim to be a healer or have any medical knowledge. I always advise they should consult their doctor.

The point of dealing with personal and collective issues and unconscious blockages is the search for integration and to become aware of ourselves as so much bigger; more creative, than we could ever imagine ourselves to be in the mundane world.

Integration implies paradox: Light and Dark, Spirit and Matter. And in my experience, it became increasingly clear that the greatest paradox in the human psyche is omnipotence and worthlessness; the interplay of standing too far forward and too far back, feeling too special and not special enough. Over the eons this has led to the prevailing ethos of humanity – dominance and servility.

The dance between the two was the lifeblood of my work, ultimately to bring the client to a place of integration in which the two are one. Like the particle and the wave both are true at the same time. We are absolutely amazing and unique, and can, at the same time, be detached enough to see it is no big deal! It is just the way it is. The realisation brings us to our most creative, most aware of our common humanity. And the promise of a 'new dawn'.

By implication the journey of consciousness is to bring awareness of spirit, the knowledge of our innate loving kindness and wisdom, right down into matter; into the human body. When it is safely part of the human framework, we will forget what hinders us most: the human predilection for addiction to drama! The drama of pain, insecurity that keeps us feeling alive.

The beautiful, joyful, touching, painful song To Be Human from the play *'Forward Together'*, says: "*If you don't know how it feels to lose, how do you know when you win? So, if it hurts to be human, count me in*". But, in the journey to evolving consciousness we see that it does not need to be like that.

* * *

After a short estrangement towards the end of my time at Le Plan, Lorna St Aubyn and I had become good friends again. As well as working at the college and Daisy Bank, Lorna had offered me a bedroom in her London house in Parsons Green, to work in once a week. It was through Lorna that I met William Davison.

William had written to her earlier that year, saying how much he admired her book *'Rituals for Everyday Living'* and wanted to discuss the idea of making a programme. Before they met, she and I watched *'Circling the Dragon'*, which William had made in China, about Deng Xiao Ping's disabled son, and was shown on BBC2. It was so good and it prompted me to say to Lorna, 'do ask him if he needs a researcher'! Although the Ritual idea never came to fruition, the result was that William came to Daisy Bank.

In the months before we met, we had both 'known' a relationship was coming up. I had been told that I would meet 'a simple gardener', a writer, who would take me to China! William just had the feeling that change was happening. His marriage had been dissolved several years earlier, and he was at the end of a fairly long-term relationship. He had two daughters.

At that time, William owned his own TV production company in Bath, specialising in programmes on disability. He had made eight series of *'Same Difference'* for Channel 4 in the eighties. But he, too, was interested in spiritual matters. It took me a while to realise he was not looking for a researcher, and was not interested in my CV, but had me down as a partner!

By that time, I had had enough of the 'agony and ecstasy' of karmic relationships – chronicled in sometimes bold detail in *'A Spot to Stand'*. But they had got me to where I was now, and I did know it would never be like that again. A month or so after my first meeting with William, I knew I was in it for the duration.

CHAPTER TWO

1996-January 1997: 14 Frome Road

'In training'

William lived in Beckington, near Bath, a forty minute drive from Stroud. Our first memorable outing was a visit to Ireland, staying in Dublin, to celebrate my birthday in July 1995. But the most exciting proposition was that we go to China, which we planned for the beginning of the following year. The 'prediction' given to me two years earlier was coming true.

Until then, for all the travelling I had done over the years, China had never appealed to me. But now I loved the idea. We devised a plan to research Chinese Gardens and put together a programme idea.

Over the last years William had made several films for various organisations, not only on disability. But by the time we met, his company was running down as he had completed his Channel Four commission. The permanent staff had left because he could hire when necessary, and eventually he had the courage to give up the office in Odd Down. He was free to explore other ideas.

I had given up working at the College and also sold my house in Stroud and moved into William's home. I did a lot of research for our trip, mainly through a marvellous book by Maggie Keswick '*The Chinese Garden*' – though of course today it is all on Wikipedia! The gardens had evolved over three thousand years, and some are still in existence today.

William contacted his counterparts in Beijing at the China Disabled People's Federation, who had worked with him on '*Circling the Dragon*'. He arranged for an interpreter and 'helper' to accompany us.

We arrived in Beijing in March 1996, and stayed at the Crown Plaza hotel, not far from the Imperial Palace and Tiananman Square. We explored Beijing, including The Summer Palace, and then travelled with our escorts, mostly by train, to see the gardens.

First, however, we went to Xian, not to miss the opportunity while in China to see The Terracotta Warriors. We also made a day trip to Qianling, about thirty-five miles from Xian - to the mausoleum of Emperor Gaozong and his Empress Wu Zetian.

I was fascinated by the Tang Dynasty (617-907) when art and culture flourished. Empress Wu all but ruled during her husband's reign and held great power as the Dowager Empress Wu after his death. The Tang Dynasty was also the golden age of Chinese gardens. After Xian, we went to Shanghai.

The Chinese garden is a landscape garden which includes both the vast gardens of the Chinese emperors and members of the imperial family - built for pleasure and to impress - and the more intimate gardens created by scholars, poets, former government officials, soldiers and merchants. These were made for reflection and escape from the outside world.

A typical Chinese garden is enclosed by walls and includes one or more ponds, rock works, trees and flowers, and an assortment of halls and pavilions within the garden. These are connected by winding paths and zig-zag galleries, and moving from structure to structure, visitors can view a series of carefully composed scenes, unrolling like a scroll of landscape paintings.

The *Yu Yuan* garden in Shanghai showed us all the elements of a classical Chinese garden. In Souzhou, where the gardens were mostly built by scholars and merchants between the 11th and 19th centuries, we visited *The Surging Wave Pavilion; The Lion Rock Garden; The Garden of the Master of the Nets; the Lingering Garden; The Humble Politicians Garden; The Garden of Harmony*. I made copious notes.

At the Embroidery Institute, which also had a garden, one of the women who came to welcome us held her hands together and bowed to me. I felt an honouring that I remember to this day, and I can now understand this Chinese custom. We made a day trip to Wuxi and Lake Tai – the birthplace of the philosophy of rock appreciation - and visited Wuxi's *Li Garden* and *Jichang Garden* in Xihui Park.

We enjoyed travelling on the Chinese double-decker trains. From Suzhou we travelled to Hangzhou, where in the Song dynasty more than fifty gardens were built on the shore of the Western Lake. We took a boat trip on the lake and visited *Ling Yin Temple (Temple of Soul's Rest)*, and *Peak Flown from Afar*, a limestone rock distinctive from the sandstone mountains all around it.

On our return to Beijing, we were a little shocked by the armfuls of souvenirs and vast expenses bills presented by our companions - which had to come out of our own pocket! But, as tradition dictates, we held a banquet for various members of the Federation, and it was fun to be amongst Chinese acquaintances.

Before leaving Beijing, we visited a Taoist temple, and on another day a driver - who we were told did not speak English - was put at our disposal for a visit to The Great Wall. We chatted freely along the way, but when I remarked that I was hot, the driver leaned forward to turn on the air-conditioning. We guessed he did speak English after all and had been 'planted'.

William's abiding memory is that in two weeks, having walked so much around the gardens, he had worn out a new and expensive pair of Swedish shoes! Our exploration of Chinese gardens had been a spectacular experience. We never did make the programme but, most important for me, I had fallen in love with China.

* * *

For four months – even during our time in China – I had been worrying about my first talk in a public forum as an established channel. Tony Neate, one of the founders and teachers of the College of Healing, asked me if I would like to give a day workshop at Runnings Park. I had attended the College in 1983, and in 1984 had written a book: *Where There's Love*: the story of the six families who had founded Runnings Park.)

I had said yes to the workshop, of course, but in truth, the thought of talking out to a group was my worst nightmare. I chose the title *'Waking up to Ourselves: communicating with other levels of consciousness'*. Tony would host the event and join me later in the day when together we would look at various ways and means of contacting 'other realms'.

I was still doing automatic writing, and far too nervous to trust myself to channel directly on the day. I did the major channelling in advance and read it as a guided meditation to the group of around thirty people, facing towards me in a large circle.

One of the major insights – through guidance – had been the concept of 'the five wounds'. As opposed to 'original sin', the guides suggested each of us came to earth carrying the 'signature' of one of these five 'original wounds.' In other words, unlike how western religions saw it, we were not born sinful but wounded.

I had been working on this concept with clients for quite a while, and it worked. The wounds were: *Betrayal, Denial, Rejection, Abuse and Abandonment.* By experiencing our particular wound; recognising it, and seeing the effect: the hurts, the misunderstandings, the anxiety this 'original wound' had caused - and which made us react to life rather than respond - these could be cleared, moved through, let go, into a new understanding of self.

After the meditation and some discussion, I went on to speak of this. And then, on the spot, directly channelled the wound for each participant in the group. Everyone seemed happy to sit quietly and reflect on their wound, until one man who was given *denial,* protested that it wasn't the right wound for him! Later, another participant told me that this was the moment when she thought 'this woman has definitely got something'!

In the afternoon, Tony and I sat together and spoke about our relationship to guidance. Tony who had been channelling HA (Helio Archaniphus) - described as a spirit guide - for many, many years, had founded a group called The Atlanteans. Over the years, he and his wife Ann, had offered a great many courses and training in psychic work.

I had loved my time at the College of Healing, which had given me a grounding, a tool kit, through which to further my own experience of healing. But it was clear to me as we spoke just how different Tony's approach to channelling was from mine, and what I felt I was doing now.

In fact, after that day, several of the participants came to see me privately. One of these, a social worker, uncovered the wound of Abuse. Extraordinary as it seemed at the time, she worked with abused children. Once we had explored fully her own sense of being abused as a child, and how it had affected the way she operated in later life, she left that line of social work. She did not 'need' it anymore.

To me channelling then was just another step along the way, the by-product of 'the feminine journey', which had begun over thirty years before. The first step, when I began to know things; had led to an awareness of the spiritual aspect of the feminine and the 'direct knowing of the Higher Self.' (Recorded in *The Wise Virgin*).

The second phase, the difficult and dark 'descent', awakened the language of the body and the Earth, during which I began the practice of etheric healing, and which coincided with my time at The College of Healing. At a later stage I became aware of the Soul as mediator between spirit and matter through the human heart. My channelling could not have manifested until these explorations – all documented in *'A Spot to Stand'* - had taken place.

Once the ordeal of the workshop was over, William and I could plan the important event of the year, our marriage! Neither of us wanted a big wedding second time around. We chose a beautiful location – Ashdown Park Hotel in the Ashdown Forest – and invited seven people to witness the day. The only family present were John and Barbara, David and Tass, William's siblings.

On my side I asked Monica and John, long-term friends who lived nearby. And Tess, who I had met in 1986 at Le Plan, and who had featured strongly in my life from then on. She gave a blessing after the ceremony as we gathered on the little wooden bridge over the lake.

The venue did us proud for the wedding breakfast, and then William and I drove to Kent for an extra celebration – with cake – at my brother Mike's house, with my mum and brother, his wife Margaret and their three children. Later we drove to Dover for an overnight stay, before catching the hovercraft to Calais for the long drive to Provence. Tess, who was now living in Abingdon, had offered us her apartment in Le Beausset – near my old home in Le Castellet.

William says now, he was impressed when, on arrival we found there had been a pretty disastrous leak, and I knew immediately who to call. Monsieur Valentini, the plumber who had saved me from several mishaps when I lived there, came and fixed it!

It was nice to show William my old haunts. The chapel dedicated to Mary Magdalene at Le Beausset Vieux, and the pottery nearby where we bought two plates – which we still use today. The coast was only six kilometers away, and William liked the pine-clad cove at Port d'Allon, which was Tess's favourite too.

I had lived in Le Castellet from 1987-1991. My place of refuge, in those days, was the wide spacious beach and harbour at St Cyr les Lecques, where I used to spend time at the end of most days. I would walk for a while, then sit and knit! The croissants in the café on the seafront at Bandol were just as good as ever. Le Castellet church, with its blue stained glass window, still held its magic. We enjoyed our time.

Of course, our relationship had its dramas. I would say for the first six years we were 'on alert', which entailed quite a lot of sparring. But eventually it settled down, and back in Beckington we began a routine. William was content because every morning we would get up, have breakfast, and then sit at the dining room table to tune-in.

William had been interested in spiritual values for some time, but in particular in past lives. The guides certainly humoured him! A significant experience for William concerned a tricky working relationship he had endured over the previous five years of his working life. He was amazed to discover that this person had featured in a past life in a less than kindly way.

Through guidance, he saw that the work colleague had been head monk in a monastery in Tibet, where William had been one of the lowly juniors. He had been picked out by this monk and used as a scapegoat to bolster himself. Despite William's position in the workplace now, this was exactly how it had felt in this life.

It is worth noting that - like me - William had the 'wound' of Rejection. During this time, he reflected that the feeling of rejection throughout his life was the reason he wished so strongly to advance the cause of disabled people.

He understood the rejection disabled people felt, and this realisation was perhaps why he could leave that work behind in due course. It was interesting to me that in our current explorations, only one life connected us - an important explanation of our being together now – but in other lives we had no link to each other at all.

Although in earlier days I had become aware of my other lives - which were important insights - I did not have the same passion now to experience past lives as William did. In these early days of working with clients, past lives came up frequently, but as the years progressed and energies changed, they became less and less significant. The deep-down issues that people faced, and which clearly bled through all their lives, could be found by delving into the current life.

Looking back, William says it was like a period of training. He seemed to slide very easily into working this way. Sometimes, when I did sessions for people *in absentia* and felt I needed confirmation, William would do the guided session alongside me as I talked into the tape, and he would 'nod' encouragement.

On one occasion, I asked him to put the difficult experience of the client through his own perceptions – with her permission. He then spoke directly on the phone to the client – who we knew very well. She was happy for him to give his sense of the situation, on her behalf.

Apart from our earlier spats, William and I laughed a lot, and still do after twenty-five years of marriage. Our relationship had a lightness of touch too. I could relax in my work because he acknowledged what I did and encouraged it. We agreed that to a greater or lesser extent our lives would be predicated on guidance.

While I was seeing clients, William was producing a monthly BBC 2 '*Learning Zone*' series for the Benefits Agency. I was also laying waste to William's garden! I had seven bonfires before the next door neighbour very politely asked if we could have a day off, for his family to visit!

It was not all work and tuning in. My brother Mike and his wife Margaret came to visit, staying at the local Woolpack pub. And at Christmas Tess took a cottage in Wales while we stayed in a nearby guesthouse. When we were there, we had lunch with Ruth White, who had also hired a cottage in Wales with her daughter Jane.

Ruth is well known for her many books and her work with her discarnate guide Gildas, and it was her seminars I attended over several years in Le Plan in the eighties. (On this occasion, she told us then that when she was married, she made fifty-two Christmas puddings for her husband; one for each week of the year!).

Back home, we often found ourselves driving past one particular house in Westbury, which we saw was for sale. We liked the look of it, but never once dreamed it was for us. But on one occasion it just suddenly clicked. It dawned on us that we could move! We arranged to look at it several times and our abiding memory is of the owner describing himself as the 'Head of Cobwebs'. We put in an offer, which was accepted, and I took over his title!

I remember early on in our relationship, William telling me he was looking for his last house, which absolutely horrified me! I could not conceive of 'settling down'. In fact, since then, including where we lived when we met, we have inhabited ten houses. Somewhere along the way William began to enjoy a change of venue almost as much as I did! We left Beckington in January 1997.

CHAPTER THREE

January 1997-August 1999: Fourways

'Adventures in self-publishing and workshops'

No sooner had we arrived at Fourways, when one morning in February I woke up in acute pain. William gathered me up and took me straight down to the GP surgery. Before he could do so, however, he had to ask the men who were cable-laying at the end of our drive to put metal plates over the hole as he needed access urgently.

The GP called an ambulance, and William drove behind it, to Bath United Hospital. Gynae and appendix consultants were called but diagnosis was unclear. We had arrived at 10am and when I finally got to the operating theatre at 8am the following morning, keyhole examination had revealed the need for an emergency appendectomy - with David a young, charming surgeon. William spent the day and night in the relatives' room – worrying.

I was in hospital, in pain, for ten days because of infection, which is when I learned I am allergic to opiates. The pain-killer Morphia was self-administered, when necessary, by pressing a button, but it caused horrendous nightly hallucinations. It was like being in a Hieronymous Bosch painting, with grotesque figures constantly dancing across my mind.

When eventually I told David, he immediately changed the method of pain relief. I confess, I also found it difficult to tolerate the Salvation Army band which came to play in the wards on Sundays. I felt so ill.

That month was William's birthday. I had pre-ordered a chocolate cake, which he and his brother John and sister-in-law Barbara - who had come to visit from Warwickshire - now had to collect. But there was also a far more important celebration. On 23rd February 1997, William's third grandchild, Toby, was born.

William, who by then had completed the *Learning Zone* series, loved Fourways. He discovered that the soil on our one-third acre of land was greensand, ideal for growing vegetables. This led to a dedication to raised-bed vegetable gardening, which has continued ever since. I liked the house, too. It had a Rayburn – which I had never had before - and a room large enough to hold workshops, if I would only take the plunge.

Just after the day at Runnings Park the year before, Tess had suggested she break me in slowly to the idea of doing workshops, and at the end of one of her own days - on the resonance of stones - she introduced me to her group as 'a special guest'. As a former geologist this extension of her interest had led to her enjoyment and experience of stones (she did not like the word crystals), as energy, and a source for healing.

Tess was now living in St Ethelwolds, a 'Benedictine initiative' begun by Dorothea Pickering. She had been invited to join as Guardian when she left her married home in Stockwell. Tess and I had been great friends and confidants since the moment we met at in 1986. She believed implicitly in the guidance and encouraged me throughout.

I had also met Tess's daughter Fran in Le Plan, with her former husband Damian. She was now married to Derek and in April 1996 their son Michael was born. Michael is my Godson, and I am inordinately proud to be so. For now, he is continuing his academic studies doing a PhD, but he has made his mark already with publications and presentations.

The following year their lovely daughter Rosie was born, and William is her honorary Godfather. She is currently studying documentary film making on social issues, a subject close to William's heart.

Tess and I did many sessions together over the years, and as the guidance changed – which I believed to be the outcome of continuous opening up to greater levels of consciousness - Tess was aware when that happened, even more than I was. She felt she made friends with the guides and was always disappointed – at first – when she perceived a change.

When she introduced me to the group, I gave each individual a short piece of guidance. By now I had stopped doing automatic writing and channelled direct. Though I did hold a pencil and 'scribble' on a notebook to anchor my concentration, which I still do today!

One participant, Jo, tells me that I gave her things she has never forgotten, one of which was that she would become an etheric healer. Jo is a physiotherapist and went on to add craniosacral and metamorphic training to her skill-base.

After the workshop she asked for a private session with me. I was no longer working at Lorna's, and Mary - a friend since I was twenty-two – had made the kindest offer for me to do readings once a month in her flat in Bloomsbury, while she was at work. Jo, who lived in Bethnal Green, became the greatest engine of my work from then on.

She recommended me to many of the clients in her own practice; people who loved her and her work. Her generous view was that she wanted as many people as possible to 'get in touch with the magic.' This built for me a substantial London clientele, and the opportunity to meet some fabulous people. When we moved to Fourways in early 1997, I would take the train from Warminster each month, and sometimes see as many as six clients in a day. I liked having a connection to London – my hometown.

Throughout the years I have depended mainly on word of mouth. I want clients to know exactly the way I work, so they can choose whether or not it feels right for them. Some people do find guided meditation difficult. It is hard to leave their heads and experience their body and feelings. For example, if the guides suggest they have a pain in the knee or a tightness in the heart (which might be a way of entering the difficulty) some clients can just 'find it', while others cannot comprehend how to do that.

Of course, the guides can just tell the client what is happening – which they sometimes have to do - but visceral experience changes the outcome more immediately. However, the influence of the guides is strangely 'powerful' and many clients who might not have imagined they could do the technique, take to it like a duck to water. Over the years I had the privilege of hearing hundreds of intimate stories.

I did not work on the phone, except with those I had already met for a face-to-face session at least once. I needed to be sure they felt safe and supported as they shared their innermost secrets and were happy to dialogue with the guides.

Apart from work, we enjoyed our travels in the next few years. Our first city excursion was to Madrid. We took the train from the main Atocha station to various places, like Avila and the famous chapel of St Theresa. On our arrival at Avila station, we looked for a bus to take us the rest of the way. William later told me he had said a little prayer at the station asking for help to get us to the chapel. Almost instantly a nun in a Nova drove past, stopped, asked where we were going, and offered us a lift!

We visited the Prada gallery and, most important, the Escorial, the royal palace of Philip II and his wife Isabella. William felt a huge interest in Philip and returned to Madrid later that year, for a week on his own to explore and research further.

We also went to Geneva - where I had lived for seven years in the early eighties, so a nostalgic visit for me. We stayed in a hotel just outside the city, on the French side, which was far cheaper, and went into Geneva by bus each day. It was good to look again at the UN agencies I had worked for, particularly the WHO, and also to revisit the slice-of-pizza lunch in the café in the Botanical Gardens.

On another occasion we took an overnight ferry to Hamburg and hired a car to drive to the Hanseatic City of Lubeck. We really liked Lubeck, which had spent decades recreating its historic centre, and was by then a UNESCO world heritage site. It was here we were introduced to stollen, which we have enjoyed every Christmas since!

We also went to Prague where, notably, we learned about the 'defenestration of Prague'. In 1618 the disgruntled Protestant estates threw two royal governors out of a window of Hradcany Castle. Typically for us, we also remember a fabulous meal in a large utilitarian café on a side street in the city.

* * *

My French friend Myrna was to marry Edouard that year, the summer of 1997, and they invited us to the wedding. She and I had met on Santorini in 1990, staying by chance at the same hotel, and as it turned out, we were both researching a novel. We had talked a lot and explored the island together.

Several years later, when we discussed our work, we discovered we had both been writing the same 'spiritual' and 'double-time' themes and including the vast volcanic eruption in

Minoan times around 1600 BC. (The result for me was *Shadowplay* - eventually published in 2013 after years of being stuck in a drawer!)

Myrna and Edouard had first met in Paris at a Greek evening class, but were now living in Valensole in the Vaucluse, in a house Edouard had inherited. Their mutual love of Greece inspired them to choose a Greek orthodox wedding in a nearby orthodox church, followed by a blessing in the Catholic church, then a formal civil marriage in the town hall the following day.

The orthodox marriage was quite an event. Myrna had asked me to be the equivalent of matron of honour. The priest performed his incantations, circling the bride and groom and significant others, but when he came to me, for whatever reason he bopped me on the nose with his bible – which was a bit of a shock!

On our return from France, William and I went to a weekend workshop in West Sussex. One of my clients who was a keen follower of Simon Peter Fuller had somehow persuaded William and I to attend his two-day workshop on the last weekend in August 1997.

Over the years, I had touched into many spiritual pathways, taken part in numerous fascinating workshops and read widely in the field, but I had never wanted to follow any other path than my own. I preferred to acquire my philosophy through my own experience, and I wanted to give my clients a unique and personal exploration of their own spiritual consciousness and creativity. My work would never consolidate into 'a teaching'.

I had not been to a workshop since my final seminar with Ruth White – on Alchemy - at Le Plan in 1989. Doing this weekend was an anomaly! Simon Peter Fuller is the founder of 'Holistic World Vision, part of a Global Network for Planetary

Transformation'. He travels the world speaking of 'spiritual re-education and awakening; of Universal Laws and Ancient Wisdom'. He also works with a group to activate earth power centres and does Power Site tours. A heavy duty Mission.

My own life and work had a smaller reach and a smaller aim. We are all light workers following our star. It is not a race, or a competition and one journey is not comparable to another. The most important word for me in this journey has been *Integrity*, and through that word I have learned to trust what I do. My life dictated that I unfolded quietly, and now I was quietly teaching.

There were thirty or forty people at Simon Peter's workshop; an astonishing number. But as soon as he began to give information handed on to him from his favourite seer, we knew it was not quite for us. Intuitively it did not tally with our own sense of guidance. So instead we just enjoyed the people we met.

The first evening was billed as an 'Essene Meal'. We had been asked to wear something white and to go barefoot. It began with Simon Peter washing our hands and our feet, and then we joined another couple at a table for four, to eat a silent meal. The small plate in front of us included a sprig of celery and some almonds. But try eating celery and almonds silently! We were so relieved when the other couple on our table started to giggle.

But our lasting memory of the workshop came on the Sunday morning, when we woke to the television news of Princess Diana's death. That morning the whole group was clearly in shock, but, extraordinarily, Simon Peter did not mention it; he simply carried on with his teaching. Until the moment, about twenty-five minutes in, when as a group we could no longer stay silent.

One by one we began to speak out about our sense of devastation. It started two or three rows in front of us and seemed to come back like a wave. Even I spoke out, which is always difficult for me. Eventually Simon Peter realised he had no option but to encompass the tragedy into his day.

Back in Fourways, like everyone else we watched Diana's hugely touching funeral on television. I was even moved to go – on my own - to St James Palace. If we needed confirmation, the guides told us she was a truly significant soul, who had changed the monarchy for ever.

The following month I began to explore my new-found love of China by taking an evening class in Mandarin at Bath College. Dexu, our Chinese teacher, taught Pinyin, a phonetic way of 'listening and speaking', without the hard task of learning characters. It is still a tough language to learn! But I was determined.

In the class I met Paz, a Peruvian woman – born in Lima - recently divorced from her Welsh husband. We became firm friends and, distance notwithstanding, remain so today. (She now lives in Nice). She had two adopted children from Columbia - which is where she met her husband - and was then living with them in Bath.

In November 1997 was the marriage of Sophia and Jeremy. I had known Sophia since 1986, when we met at Le Plan. She was part of the core group set up by Lorna to ensure the smooth running of the seminars. By coincidence, or synchronicity, we had earlier both seen an astrologer in Connecticut, who told each of us we would meet! At that time, we were both interested in the significance of Mary Magdalene who was associated with Provence.

Sophia is French/Polish, brought up in Brazil and speaks four languages. In all ways she is hugely gifted. She and I have the same birthdate and our numerology is the same, despite nine years difference in age. I later introduced her to Myrna, and we decided it was like being sisters. (I was big Sis to them both!) Myrna, as an English teacher, also had perfect English.

When we met, Sophia was married to Peter; they had come to work in Le Plan as a couple. Now divorced, she was to marry Jeremy, who at that time worked in public relations for a trade union, and we were honoured to be among the few invited guests. These included Sophia's brother Paul, who had turned up unexpectedly; Jeremy's fifteen year old son Jake from his previous marriage, and their seven year old daughter Isabella - who was a little non-plussed that Sophia was not wearing a white dress.

The wedding was in St David's in Wales, and after the civil ceremony at the Warpool Court Hotel we walked to St Non's cave. St Non's, near a sacred spring, was a Christian retreat, where she was supposed to have given birth to St David.

Jake as master of ceremonies invited Paul, William and I to the front each to give a blessing. The night before in a London hotel, Paul had had a dream. When he woke up, he looked at the note he had made and found it was a blessing from the elements! When Sophia reminded him of this recently, this highly respected Californian Maths professor was shocked. It was not his scene.

William spoke, and I read a blessing from the guides before we returned to the hotel for the wedding meal. At some point during the weekend we went for an excursion, and driving through the coastal town of Fishguard, we passed the house we would move to several years later! But at that point, nothing could have been further from our minds.

* * *

My first three books, written in the seventies, had been accepted by publishers, where all the practical things, like costs, marketing and PR are taken care of. All the author had to do was write the book and then, during the printing process, read the galley proofs. But over Christmas and early into the following year, 1998, William and I embarked on a crazy plan to self-publish. We felt it would be the simplest way to release a channelled book.

Day after day we did sessions together, recording them for me to edit and type up later. In those days, books were still published through the printing process. We chose William's photo of a Day Lily for the cover design and sent all the material for *'Making the Most of the Life You've Got: a manual for the new millennium'* to our chosen printer in Whitstable. We went there several times to oversee the process.

To make it more difficult for ourselves we decided to include two audio cassette tapes with each book, in a specially made pack. These were more like an instruction manual through guided mediations.

Even though William enjoyed the tape-making side – he was a sound engineer in the early days – it was a mad undertaking. We realised that our marketing skills left much to be desired – and still do. But the book did sell – mainly to my 'constituency' clientele which was expanding considerably. So, all in all we were satisfied.

In 1998, we also published under Rowan Communications, a book for Tess: *'The Everlasting Relationship: Mother and Child at War and Peace'*. For Tess the changing relationship between mother and child was the most fundamental change of the New Millennium. We were singing from the same hymn sheet, but Tess was focussed in a different way.

In these testing times, she said, the tyranny of the child is a direct reaction to the age-old tyranny within the mother herself. It was her contention that the underlying need for outer change is a need for the Collective Mother – of whom all men and women are part - to redefine our relationship to our own inner child, or Soul, and thus to release a profound new level of freedom, creativity and peace.

* * *

I remember Lorna St Aubyn and I, in 1991, sitting at the back of a meeting in honour of Sir George Trevelyan, who was retiring from the Wrekin Trust. This was the spiritual education foundation he had initiated in 1971 concerned with spiritual nature of humanity in a non-sectarian way.

For some reason she and I had remarked to each other that thank goodness we would never have to hold workshops. We agreed that nothing could be more terrifying. But at the beginning of 1998, shortly after publication of '*Making the Most*,' I embarked on just the thing I feared most. My workshop life began with a series of weekends based on the book.

My earlier books – under my maiden name Annie Wilson - had been well received, so in a small way I felt 'known' in the field. But I now worked as Annie Davison, and those earlier people would not know who I was. The workshops now drew mainly from my new clients and their recommendations.

My hand had been held by Tony Neate at Runnings Park. And, somehow, by word of mouth, several people, like Glen, Lisa, Hilary and particularly Elisabeth and James, who had attended the healing and channelling courses there, ended up with me. Tess in Abingdon, who had made it her mission to encourage me earlier, would now come to my workshops, and brought several of her friends with her.

In January, Tess and I ran a day together at All Saints Vicarage in Battersea. But on February 14th, 1998, I was on my own - about to launch the first of numerous workshops and courses over the next two decades, in many different locations.

My work was based on my sense that there was now beginning a spiritual awakening that defied everything we have known and understood so far. Others have described it as a 'paradigm shift'. Astrologers like Lorna Bevan have talked of our move from 3D to 5D consciousness.

I wanted to teach everything I knew to those who were feeling the confusion of this changing world. To show that by releasing the old misconceptions of ourselves as victims to the past, reacting unconsciously to personal and collective history, we can move towards a renewal. In Lorna's terms, to teach the 4D route to 5D consciousness, where ultimately, we can experience the magnificence of what it is to be human at a much deeper, universal level. Pure creativity and choice can replace reactive programmed behaviour.

The work for me is an evolutionary process. I don't have a standard repertoire and have never repeated a topic. We all just roll on together. But in the beginning, I micro-managed each workshop in a way I would not dream of doing today. The day before, I would sit with William and plan the day meticulously; asking the guides for a blow by blow itinerary. I would write the order of play on a card; two sessions in the morning, two in the afternoon, lunch to share, and two tea breaks. I would even practise some of the programme with William as a pretend participant.

I kept to my script: to introduce the day; ask the participants to say a little about themselves; before a quiet moment. And then two channelling sessions - with me filling in the gaps for explanations, as the sense of the day emerged.

The group sessions were not unlike client work. With a general theme, each participant would be addressed individually while the rest of the group would hold their own experience, *and* tune into the other stories. I don't know how they did that, but they always did!

If someone was struggling, the guides might ask another participant to help. For people at the beginning of their journey it could be traumatic and lonely to face their fears, perhaps even shame and guilt - especially in public. But the group experience, and chats in between, brought explanation and resolution; to know there is meaning in our lives and meaning in the things that happen.

Even when facing the deepest, sometimes painful truths, the group sessions were kindly, light and often humorous. No matter how serious a subject they tackled, the guides had a lightness of touch, a humour of spirit. I remember the guides suggesting to one client that she should imagine herself knitting her left and right sides together (showing her that she was at that moment out of balance). After the session she said; 'did you know I was a knitting pattern designer?'

I also know the group felt they were in a safe space. That year we covered topics from *'Making the Most'*: such as *'The Soul Wound'*; *'Releasing Money'* - in which they experienced a different sense of abundance - and *'Tuning into Nature'*.

William and I had also published another channelled book: *'The Woman Who No Longer Knows: An A-Z of the changing relationship between men and women'*. This suggested that the balance of power must realign, from, dependence to independence to interdependence. Women were being asked to release the 'warrior' in favour of the 'receiving woman', who is able to receive 'all that is' - within. A workshop *'New Relationship'* coincided with publication in March.

Eventually, after several years, I had the courage not to plan at all. I let the guides lead where they would, confident it would be in the right direction, and exactly what each person needed. The participants of the workshops changed over the years, of course, but many who were there at the beginning remain interested in the work to this day, and we have become friends.

To be known in this way and appreciated for what I do is such a privilege. Of course, I have friends from the past who have no idea what I do, and never ask. I don't mind that at all. In fact, I like it. I remember in Le Plan a young man participant saying: 'the spiritual journey is 'caught not taught'.

I have never had a 'mission to explain', but if someone does ask, I will do my best – trying not to sound too 'weird'. I remember one cousin who, when she came to visit us in Fourways, announced in front of the guests: 'But it's all nonsense, isn't it'? And she hasn't changed her mind since!

In the early summer of that year William took a two-month break to write up his material on Philip II. He drove to Provence to stay in Tess's apartment in Le Beausset, but on arrival found that smoke infiltration from a fire in an apartment below had made the ceiling black! Before settling down to work, he had to wash the ceiling several times and give it several coats of emulsion. By strange chance, he also met Myrna's husband Edouard, who was staying with family nearby.

I was enjoying becoming part of the Davison family: most of whom I met at the annual family Golf Day, held at Biddenham Golf Club. The event was spearheaded by William's mum, then in her nineties, and living in a care home. I could see how feisty she must have been, as the matriarch of the family.

Golf Day was a keenly competitive event, with family honour at stake! John and Tass, William's older siblings and their children, and several cousins were keen players, but it did not quite suit William's temperament. Still, we always enjoyed the lunch! And the day faded away soon after Mrs Davison died in 2000.

Being a step-mother – to Emma and Mel – and step-grandmother to seven grandchildren (all Emma's) was a little out of my range. When we lived at Fourways there were three: Lauren, 4; Immy 3; and Toby 2. They were blond and bouncy and gorgeous. Em and James were a large and tight family unit, and still are, and we have watched avidly as the grandchildren, now mostly in their twenties, have grown and made their way in life.

Fourways was near to Salisbury Plain, and we walked there regularly. The house itself was large enough to have visitors. The children and grandchildren were close enough to pop down to see us, and Sophia and Jeremy came to stay. My long-term friend Hannah, who had lived in Norfolk and was now in Australia, came to visit before she left. My mum and aunt came for Christmas.

But there was always a nagging concern for me – the threat of a by-pass. Several proposals had been in the works for years, but so far nothing had been agreed. Now the clamour was louder and for one particular route. If this came to fruition, it would take the by-pass in a wide arc around our house.

We joined the protest, and stood with others outside the council offices, holding our banner and making our feelings known. It clearly did not go down well locally, because one morning a brick was thrown through our car window. The anxiety was always there, but by then we were ready to move and had put the house on the market. Ironically, the by-pass was never built.

In early 1999, while waiting for a sale, I began another half-year series of one-day weekend workshops: '*Relationship and Change*', described as 'an opportunity to learn to shift gear on every level, to make a new relationship to yourself, to others, and to the magnificent world we live in'. Two of these workshops were held at Tess's home in Abingdon.

In June we finally sold our house. It had taken a long time, but in the end was bought by a young couple who had known the house and liked it since childhood. Then, at the last minute, there was a major hiccough when the chain behind us fell through: our buyers had been let down.

Although it was only a matter of days before things were back on track, in that time our intended house in West Overton near Marlborough had been re-sold, and we had two weeks to find something else. With little choice - and although not quite our style - we decided on High View, a bungalow in Elcot Lane, Marlborough. It was within walking distance of the town centre, opposite the sewage works - or water meadows!

But before we moved, in July that year Paz and I went for a month to Beijing, for a summer course in Mandarin at the Beijing Capital Normal University. Our year of evening classes at Bath College had ended but we had both caught the bug.

Beijing at forty degrees plus was unbearably hot! Paz, from South America, was in her element. Each night I had to plead with her to turn on the air conditioning, while she snuggled under a duvet to keep warm. In the morning she would run around the university athletics track, while there were times I could barely walk, my legs turned so blotchy and red with the heat.

But it was the best experience; and we loved it. We teamed up with an American woman who as often as she could, persuaded us to go to McDonalds! She had been teaching

English near Shanghai but missed the burgers. We also learned from a fellow student, Miranda, how to dodge traffic on five lane Beijing highways.

And it was here in the University that we met and became friends with Lizi Hesling. Less than half our age, Lizi, originally from Cornwall, was doing Mandarin full time. She had studied Chinese for three years at Edinburgh University, and was now planning to take up life in China. We remained friends for many years.

* * *

I had left William at home to do the packing up! And in August 1999 we moved to High View.

CHAPTER FOUR

August 1999-January 2003: High View

'Full-on'

At 4am on our first morning in High View I woke William and said, 'it's no good, we've got to have another kitchen'. This decision set the trend. In twenty-five years and ten houses, we have spent a lot of time refurbishing and re-decorating, including installing four kitchens ourselves. It became a large part of our activity and enjoyment.

We made houses in the way we wanted them, but other people seemed to like what we had done. We always enjoyed going back to our old homes to see what the new owners had done to improve on our work; which they always did.

Early on at High View, when David Furlong brought his seven year old daughter Lily to see us, she quickly pointed out that the paint along the coving was very wobbly. After that it was decided that William would roller the major part of a room, and the top and bottom lines would be left to me! We settled down into an acceptable division of labour. For example, in all the houses I did the gardening while William grew the vegetables.

David Furlong and his former wife Diane were two of the original six founder-members and tutors at Runnings Park, when I attended the first College of Healing. David and I were now friends. He even took up residence in High View the week before we arrived, as he needed somewhere to stay before settling down in Marlborough himself.

David's passion was, and is, earth mysteries. His book in 1997 *'Keys to the Temple'* was an intensively researched book unravelling the mysteries of the ancient world: pyramids, ley patterns, the Mayans. Just after we moved, he invited me to take part in his advanced course for Feng Shui consultants.

He knew my interest in Chinese gardens and his suggestions for ways in which I might work in this group, included an experiential session on China's spiritual system and what it means to us now. And, given that Chinese art was designed as a spiritual and heart-opening experience for people, we decided on a session for opening the heart and understanding why, in our woundedness, this has been so difficult to do. Finally, in relation to Feng Shui, I would do an experiential session on clearing the inner clutter; as important as re-ordering our external mode of living.

This September workshop was held in the Jubilee Centre in Marlborough High Street, which during the week was a day centre for the over-sixties. Once again the workshop was pushing my comfort zone, but the day was successful, and one or two of David's feng shui consultants later came to see me. He and I did several workshops together, so I got to know his group well, some of whom eventually attended my own workshops.

Sometime later, Jeremy and Sophia, William and I went – almost on a pilgrimage – to Monks' House, in Rodmell, East Sussex, where Virginia and Leonard Woolf had lived in the early twentieth Century. They had bought the house in 1919 for seven hundred pounds and moved there permanently in 1940 when their flat in Bloomsbury was destroyed in an air raid. Virginia committed suicide in 1941 by drowning herself in the River Ouse nearby.

William and I had recently visited Charleston in Firle, the home of Virginia's sister Vanessa Bell, and in my younger years, my imagination had been totally captured by The Bloomsbury Group. I had read many of the fascinating biographies of these associated writers, artists, intellectuals and philosophers: my favourite being Virginia.

I remember with pleasure meeting the artist Diana Lodge. Then in her eighties she was one of the guests for the HTV series *'Inner Journeys'*, on which I was the researcher in 1992. Diana and her husband author and poet Oliver Lodge had been on the fringe of the Bloomsbury Group. An original painting by her that I bought at the time and still have today, is of her cottage kitchen in Stroud. On the wall over the woodburning stove, you see a portrait of her in her younger days - painted by Bloomsbury heavyweight Duncan Grant.

The Saturday workshops *'Relationship and Change'* continued to the end of 1999. We explored the confusion of inner and outer change, with the opportunity to learn to shift gear on every level; to make a new relationship to ourselves and others. The later workshops linked these changes to the New Millennium, showing how it was possible to 'reincarnate' in this life on a different vibrational level.

In mid-December I went for a week to France – travelling by train and then bus – to visit Myrna. She and Edouard had now parted, and Myrna had bought a *cabanon*, amongst the olive trees, a short distance from their married home in Valensole. It was the first of many annual visits, which I loved, and on this occasion, Sophia came for a day, too. She drove from her parents' home near Nice.

The following year, in March 2000, Janice Dolley, initiator of the Bridge Trust, invited me to do an experiential workshop for her members at her home in Warwickshire. The subject was *'the changing levels of consciousness'*; how best to respond as individuals and how to best serve as the Bridge Trust.

The Bridge Trust was an association for building bridges from old consciousness to new; through a small organic farm, an educational centre and many other ventures. Since the seventies Janice had worked tirelessly towards what she described as 'unity awareness'; and amongst other things was concerned with bringing consciousness to mainstream Christianity. For thirty years an educator at the Open University, I had been introduced to her by Tess in the 1980s. At one point I had asked her to recommend a film maker for a project I was working on at the WHO in Geneva.

Over the years I did other work apart from my own. In 1997, a senior social worker and long-term client, who was taking a play therapy course, had asked her governing body if I could be her supervisor. They agreed, and over the course of a year I worked with her, through guidance, on behalf of various children in her care.

Later when she went on assignment to Rumania, she consulted me about a child in a difficult orphanage setting. And another long-term client invited me to work with her radionics practitioner committee group; to move them through what appeared to be a 'stuck moment'.

In 2000, I also embarked on another new enterprise. *'Waking Up to Integrity: a school of channelling and understanding spiritual morality'*. This four-weekend course aimed to help each individual wake up to their highest creative voice, in whichever way it would manifest, (channelling being only one possible manifestation). They stayed in local B & Bs and brought lunch to share.

It was a lovely group of nine participants, the maximum I preferred for any workshop. I particularly remember Sophia, of course, and Elisabeth McCrae, who would also become a special friend. Anya, a young garden designer who lived in Marlborough and was a client of David Furlong; Jonathan, a gifted sculptor from West Sussex; Joy, a local environmentalist, and Julia, whose brother I had helped at the College of Psychic studies.

In September I ran a further one-day workshop on our most recent book: *'The Woman Who No Longer Knows'*. This was in London - at my friend Jan's in Southfields. I have known Jan since our journalism days in the seventies, and she and her husband Barrie have always been welcoming no matter what. On this occasion they were away on holiday.

Jan's house was convenient for the London constituency, and it was there I met 'the babies', thanks to Jo. Three lovely young women in their twenties: Claire, Anna and Kelly, who were so bright, so 'on message', it was a delight. I still have contact with Anna and Claire, now in their forties and married with children. They came to more workshops over the years – and still do – though Claire is now in Australia. They are still amazing superstars!

At Christmas that year my mum came to stay. My mum and I got on well, and these days talked a lot on the phone. In the mid-nineties my brother Mike had persuaded her to leave her home in Finchley to be nearer him and his family in Kent. She was never keen – especially when it meant leaving her beloved garden – but she agreed to move to a wardened flat.

Now, when we collected her, we knew she was ill, but not quite how ill because she had still not been diagnosed. She slept on a bed set up in our dining room, and I did have to help her with showering and hair-washing, but I shall always remember how perky she looked in her bright red dress on Christmas Day. Tess was there too.

At New Year she was reluctant to go home, but we had to take her back for a scheduled endoscopy. I remember how frightened she was, but we were there then. After the procedure, we left her at my brother's house, and, still not understanding how bad it was, continued with our plan for a short holiday with Tess in Nerja, Southern Spain.

I told Mike I would phone every day, which I did. And three days into our holiday he said: 'you'd better come quickly'. Leaving William and Tess, I caught a BA flight back to London the following day and phoned as soon as I got back to Victoria Station in the late afternoon. I was ready to take a train to Maidstone, when Mike answered and said the devastating words: 'you're not welcome here. And if you come down you won't stay in mum's flat'.

All I could do was get myself home, and then collapsed on the floor in shock. My mum died that night, a week before her ninetieth birthday, asking where I was. William and Tess returned from Spain a few days later as planned.

My brother and his family – who had no idea how close I was to my mum – declared that I had let my mother down and they allowed me no input into her funeral. Although I did attend – which I was not inclined to do - I went under my own steam and sat at the back with Mary and William.

Later, with Tess, we held our own 'memorial', in the sitting room at High View. I imagined we were in Chartres cathedral, and we played music I thought my mum would like. Each of us spoke our mum memories. Later I planted a yellow rose in our garden.

Mike and I were estranged for eleven years – only his elder daughter Karen stayed in touch throughout, for which I was really grateful. I could look back to her wedding to David Gray in 1995, when they had been married in Bearsted Church near Maidstone, on a lovely hot day in July. The reception was held in the Lime Tree in Lenham, Kent, and Mary, my mum and I had sat together.

It was only when my sister-in-law Margaret died in 2011, that it became clear that it was she who had instigated the estrangement. From that point on, my brother came to stay with us virtually every three or four months, in our various houses, and we got on very well. But until then we had no further contact.

I began a second four-weekend School of Channelling in December 2000, until May 2001. This particular course spawned some lovely friendships. Sophia, living then in Berkhamsted, came again, with her friend and client, Susan, from Tring. Elisabeth came again, too, and Gill was there, from Le Plan days. She now lived in East Sussex.

Brenda was from Suffolk, and Barbara from Wales. They had both been clients since that first workshop at Runnings Park. Brenda had told me later that she had woken up one morning with the name Annie Wilson in her head and, asking around, had found the workshop. She has been a client and friend ever since.

I speak of these friends in particular because they have stayed the course, but there were many others who over the years came to work with me. There were men clients too, like Philip, who was always enthusiastic about the work, and grateful for what he had learned, but over the years it became clear that my constituency was mainly women.

I did a one-day follow-up to the Channelling courses and continued to work one day a month at Mary's in Bloomsbury. It was still a busy practice. At first, I would stay overnight with Jan and Barrie. Later – and for many years - I stayed with Eileen in East Barnet, so I could do 'this and that' for her as she grew more elderly.

In 2001 I also started weekly Mandarin lessons with a young Chinese woman, Wang, in Swindon. We became friends and she and her husband Gong and their eight year old daughter – who loved Harry Potter - would sometimes come to tea. Eventually they moved to Burgess Hill, for Gong's job as a water engineer.

We had good relationships with our nearest neighbours: Bill and Daphne – who were highly amused at the 'goings on' in our house. And Richard Shirley-Smith, a classical artist, well known in his rarefied field. Richard was always longing for a live-in relationship and had been pursuing society portrait painter, Rosemary, for many years. In the meantime, we three had lots of tea and ice cream together.

Our time at High View was the busiest we had known. Soon after we arrived, I sat at the kitchen table for four months to write my 'autobiography': '*A Spot to Stand*'. My aim was to cover 'the journey so far': from 1970-1995; one I described as not wishing on my worst enemy. The stages of life in this first memoir were based on relationships that moved me through the unknown and unknowable of the spiritual 'call'. I had copious notes, letters and diaries. It lay in a drawer until 2017.

During our time there, I heard that my long-time friend Chris Nixon had died. I was notified by his friend Jock, who I had lodged with in Kew in the seventies. I had known Chris since my days on '*Petticoat*' in the early seventies. '*Petticoat*' was a national magazine for young people – a rival to '*Jackie*'. Amongst other things I wrote a film column as well as celebrity profiles, and Chris, as a unit film publicist, would invite me to locations to interview his stars.

We became friends and it was he who first called me Annie rather than Anne - which has stuck ever since - and over the years we would meet for lunch in London from time to time.

Once or twice I would act as hostess for the launches of his coffee table books on motor-racing. One in particular I remember was on Aston Martin, held in their plush showrooms.

His death was a shock, particularly for the circumstances he was found in. He lived alone in his flat in Richmond – he had never married – and was found five days after his death, which is hard to contemplate.

William and I attended his funeral at the Mortlake Crematorium, with several people from the racing world, including Sir Stirling Moss, Britain's well-known Formula 1 driver. During the eulogy, we laughed when Jock said, 'We all remember our friend Chris. He was a 'miserable sod!', which lanced a feeling of great sadness. We then went to a pub by the river for the wake.

On 30th March 2002 the Queen Mother died. My friend Linda was visiting from America, and mainly for her benefit we went to Westminster Abbey. We queued with many others, to file past the Queen Mother's coffin and pay our respects.

I had known Linda since 1978. We had met at a yoga class given by Lilla Bek at the home of Baron and Baroness Di Pauli in St John's Wood. I had a room in the house (where I wrote Lilla's book '*What Colour Are You?*') and later Linda took a room, too. She was a Eurythmist - the Rudolf Steiner based system of movement and speech.

She had trained at Emerson College in East Sussex, and then, in the 1980s, when she went to study at the Goetheanum in Dornach, Switzerland and I was working as an editorial consultant for WHO in Geneva, we could meet quite often. I went to Dornach for her final performance exams.

After various posts in UK Steiner schools, she returned to the States, and I visited her several times: twice in Santa Fe, once in Hershey, Pennsylvania where, amongst other things, we did an official tour of the Hersey Chocolate factory! And then Mechanicsburg, where she later moved to be closer to her parents, who were then in a retirement village. She now lives and works in New York.

2002 was a busy year for William, too. He had written a programme idea, loosely based on 'promoting Britain'. He sent it to the advertising magnate Sir Martin Sorrell, and Sir Martin replied! He said that a venture he supported in Shanghai 'Sporting Frontiers', was thinking along the same lines.

On the off-chance in April that year, William went to Shanghai and set up a meeting with Jonty Kelt, the marketing man. A fee was agreed for *'British Adventure',* a six-month project which went into production in London a month or so later.

The idea was that publicity films produced by the British Government would be introduced by a well-known Chinese TV presenter, Yuan Ming, who had spent three years at Cambridge. Sponsorship came from corporates like Virgin, Chivas Regal Whisky, De Beers, B & Q, and each of these companies took part. Vivien Westwood and Burberrys were also amongst the sponsors. The whole series would be dubbed into Chinese for Shanghai Television.

Filming itself, mostly in London, involved William, his Australian camera man (part of the Sporting Frontiers team) and Ming. It also took the team to Scotland, to the Chivas distillery, and the river Spey nearby, which led to a serendipitous film of Ming learning to fish.

The Virgin segment, filmed on 1 August 2002, highlighted a thirty-minute inaugural flight – with Sir Richard Branson - of the latest wide-bodied aircraft (the A360-600) which took off from Heathrow and landed at Farnborough. For Vivien Westwood, Ming wore a dress from the fashion house; but otherwise her wardrobe was supplied by Burberrys. They also filmed on the Houses of Parliament tea terrace.

At the end of filming, we were was invited to a celebratory dinner at a smart restaurant in London, and I was introduced to Jonty and the team. With the London work complete, William then spent three weeks in Melbourne, supervising the editing. This meant he could meet Hannah, who was working there at the time.

By then, Tess had moved from Abingdon to Fishguard in Wales. She had bought a large rural property, Cefn-y-Dre, next to a working farm, with the dream of opening a Spiritual Education Centre. Her greatest wish was that her daughter Fran, husband Derek and their two children – who at the time were part of a community near Oxford - would join her. In August, while William was in Melbourne, I did a five-day workshop in her home: '*Landscape of the Soul*'.

During my own spiritual journey, 'Spirit of Place' had always been important. The sense that where I lived – and the energy of that land – mirrored the stage of the journey I was at. But even though we now moved so much, it no longer felt that the land on which I lived was significant in the same way. But in this workshop, I wanted the participants to explore their own personal landscapes, as soul consciousness became entwined with personality. Also, to envision the places that were best for their new creativity: to see where they lived in a new light.

In these early workshops I seemed to do a lot of 'emergency' individual sessions, if people opened up to difficult material that they could not resolve in the group and needed individual attention. We also had one or two excursions.

As usual, William and I were ready to move on. We put High View on the market and - to our own surprise - on a visit to Tess made an offer on a house in the main street of Fishguard!

But before we moved, several months later, we had several adventures.

To begin with, I went to Beijing for a few weeks on my own to study Mandarin – yet again. This time at the Foreign Affairs College. This raised things to a whole new level! The students were all much younger than me, and although there were one or two other westerners, most were from Mongolia. They had already had to learn English to do this class. The course was tough going because for the first time I had to learn characters as well as Pinyin, which was like learning two languages side by side.

It was nice in the college. The room was fine – only seven pounds a day - and the meals okay. A few weeks into the course there was an 'open day' event, and one Saturday morning we formed a small part of a big College parade - marching in front of several military men sitting at a table.

One of our students stood at the front of our group holding a banner, and then we were off, chanting over and over again: '*Yi, er, san, ce.* (One, two, three, four). *Learning Chinese is the best thing since sliced bread*' (or something like that!) as we marched all the way round the parade ground. When we passed the military table, the men burst out laughing! We were the only foreign students.

We were asked by the teachers if anyone would be interested to do some work outside the course. Some students were paid two hundred yuan (twenty pounds) a lesson to teach English, while I offered to do some editing for an English-speaking website. I worked one evening a week with a Chinese girl called Jane – the chief designer – to get the language operationally correct.

But the Mandarin course nearly killed me! My head got more and more loaded, with the lesson in the day and trying to learn the characters and match them to the phonetics at night. When William arrived, he saw I was completely exhausted and decreed that 'enough is enough'! We saw the principal, who told us it was always more difficult for older students, and I left!

While working on '*British Adventure*', William had been in touch with the French director of Handicap International in Beijing, who said he was looking to make a programme in Tibet, similar to William's UK Channel 4 series, '*Same Difference*'. This is why William was here, to bring a sample VHS tape.

We both stayed in the college for a few more days and then returned home, but it was only a matter of weeks before William was to embark on the Tibetan film.

HI wanted films on three topics. Artificial limbs were only available for the whole of Tibet at the Handicap International Clinic in Lhasa, and they wanted to promote this on Tibetan TV. They were also providing money and expert support to deaf people, to enable them to produce a dictionary in Tibetan of universal sign language, which had not been formalised before. Thirdly, they wanted to promote an outreach care programme where health professionals, travelling on HI motorbikes, visited and supported families with a disabled child.

In September we flew to Shanghai, and apart from calling in to see Sporting Frontiers, we then flew directly, via Chengdu, to Lhasa. These days there is a train journey which will help visitors acclimatise slowly to the altitude, but for us, going from low elevation to twelve thousand feet (3656 meters) was a shock. More so for William.

As he walked down the steps of the plane and across the run-way, he realised he could hardly breathe! It was a scary experience. This was followed by an intense headache. When we arrived at our hotel, he was offered an oxygen pillow with a nose piece and immediately felt better.

I didn't notice the altitude at all, and I wondered, on reflection, if this could be because I had suffered from acute asthma from the age of two to thirteen. Perhaps I had become acclimatised to not being able to breathe, and maybe something in my lungs – or my brain - had been altered?

Lhasa is a small town, and William could easily walk to Handicap International, housed in a traditional Tibetan office decked in red drapes. The camera crew were from Tibetan Television, and Jigme, a staff member of HI, was his interpreter. At the beginning, Jigme virtually ignored William, but it improved as time went on. It was only at the end, at a dinner William gave for the crew, that Jigme told him that Tibetans hated the English, because a hundred years ago English soldiers had machine-gunned the Tibetan army.

William spent time researching before filming began. In the prosthetic clinic and workshop an expert prosthetist - a Belgian volunteer - was making the artificial limbs. The HI team had persuaded a beggar without limbs to have prosthetics made and to be filmed in the process of construction and fitting.

The man was the perfect interviewee. He said all the right things to camera and that he looked forward to going back to the family farm now he could walk. But when the filming stopped and he was reassured they were pleased with the result, he said that actually he would go back to begging, because he made more money! He would have to take the legs off!

William was touched most by filming the difficulties of life in the countryside. The scenes of a mother who worked in the fields, whose child had muscular dystrophy, and of the social worker arriving by motorbike, talking and offering counsel.

One Sunday we were both invited to the deaf club. We had been told that every visitor must bring a game, so on the evening before we bought Mars bars from our hotel and wrapped them in layers of newspaper. Our game was to be 'pass the parcel'. Because the club members could not hear music, we turned the light on and off instead. When the Mars bar finally emerged, the winner insisted it was cut up into tiny pieces so everyone could have a share.

During this enchanting visit, we were offered small plastic cups of yak butter tea. We each had a new cup, where we knew they normally had to be shared. I really disliked the tea but drank it, of course, knowing how precious and honouring this was.

What touched me most was out in the field when the deaf young women, in beautiful traditional costume, began to dance. Their leader played a cassette and waved her hands in rhythm, to which they danced and moved their arms in perfect time. It made me cry. At the end of our visit we were asked to edit the English introduction to their new sign language dictionary.

While William worked, I walked around Lhasa. Near to our hotel was the Jokang temple where the pilgrims prostrated themselves along the ground to this sacred site, which the Tibetans considered their most sacred temple. I could walk to The Potala, a dzong fortress, the winter palace of the Dalai Lama from 1649 to 1959, since when it has been a museum and was made a world heritage site in 1994.

Our favourite café in Llasa was the Dunya, a joint Tibetan/Dutch venture. This was near another restaurant we liked, which had a little cabin at the end where you could watch - while eating - the head lice lady picking nits for the locals! If not walking, we travelled by bicycle rickshaw, although when William started editing the film at Tibetan Television, he rode to work on the back of Jigme's motorbike.

We stayed for the whole six weeks at the Flora Hotel in the Muslim quarter, owned by the nicest, most charming man, who came from Nepal every year to run the hotel. We were within hailing distance of the mosque and were woken every morning by the call to prayer. Outside there was a bustling market.

On one occasion the prosthetics team took us on an excursion in their 4 x 4 - the roads outside Lhasa were really rocky. We saw several monasteries, local sites - and road gangs where the men smoked, and the women did the heavy load work.

Towards the end of our stay, we visited the Lhasa carpet factory, where rows of women, seven to a bench, were weaving the most fabulous rugs on a hand loom. The factory exported traditional rugs all round the world, and of course we bought one, and had it shipped home.

But our best outing was to Namtso Lake (the Heavenly Lake). The Handicap International driver took us 240 kilometers north of Lhasa, to this highest saltwater lake in the world, at nearly fourteen thousand feet. We spent the morning walking round the lake, which was awash with prayer flags. A fitting ending to our time in Tibet

And finally, in January 2003 we moved to Fishguard.

CHAPTER FIVE

January 2003-December 2003: Alt Wen

'Not our finest hour'

When we purchased Alt Wen - which we renamed Rowan House after our publishing venture - our plan had been to buy a small pied-a-terre in London, too; not to lose touch with civilisation! We had even found a small town house in Winchmore Hill, but in the end decided against the extravagance of taking on a mortgage. So, rather unexpectedly, we landed hook, line and sinker in Fishguard, in the former ferry Captain's house.

We decided we would manage the move ourselves. William had hired a van and made a couple trips beforehand, helped by two local men on arrival. But on moving day there was one unforeseen circumstance: our sofa was too big to go through the front door! We hauled it back into the van and took it, with the two matching armchairs, to the local tip! Fortunately, they were then donated to a charity.

We bought a smaller suite, thanks to Peggy Smallbone's generous house-warming gift. Peggy is a long story. In 1976 I met Vlyn McNeil, in the village of Holford, Somerset, where I was 'in retreat' over Christmas, at a friend's cottage. I had just returned from a three month voyage on *The Lindblad Explorer*, with my then partner Lyall Watson, and was now planning my first book.

Immediately I arrived in Holford, Vlyn had gathered me up and included me in her Christmas celebrations. And in Spring 1977, she and her husband John, offered me a room in their house as the writing place for *'The Wise Virgin'*. For many years after that, she was my 'go to' friend for solace, comfort and fun. (Vlyn was passionate about astrology, and it was she who indoctrinated me into this art – almost by osmosis – which led me to my own study of astrology in the nineties.)

In later years, divorced from John, she landed in Bovey Tracey, a near neighbour to Peggy Smallbone, who became her closest friend. I would visit them in Bovey and also for Christmas meals at their favourite holiday place in Dorset.

Vlyn, who was nineteen years older than me, died in 2003, and I felt that Peggy and I had 'inherited' each other. I continued to visit Peggy as often as I had visited Vlyn, until her own death in 2011.

Alt Wen had been left in a fairly parlous state. Over the coming year we decorated throughout, installed central heating, had the place rewired and made a new kitchen. We also turned an outside loo into an inside cloakroom, wonderfully assisted by our nice new next door neighbour John. The Clutterbucks, who lived on the other side, were also charming, if eccentric.

From the back garden we had a marvellous view of the sea, and the crossing of the ferry set the time of day. It passed on its way into the harbour at 12.15 and left for Rosslare in Ireland at 2.15. On the day the ship had engine trouble and did not run for a few days, we felt that time had ceased.

Turning right outside our house, we could walk directly down the street to the harbour and our favourite café, or take the long way along the coastal path around the town. If we turned left, we could walk to a sheltered cove, past the house once occupied by the broadcaster Wynford Vaughan-Thomas.

One advantage of living near the harbour was that in June, on our wedding anniversary, we walked down to catch the ferry to Ireland. On arrival in Rosslare, we climbed up the hill to the hotel for a celebration dinner and stayed the night. Next morning, we caught the ferry back to Fishguard and walked home. We loved the simplicity of it.

We were on the border between North and South Wales, and the change from English to Welsh speaking locals. We learned quickly that this was an important distinction. The wife of Tess's farming neighbours told us that although she was born only a mile and a half away, on the English side, she was never quite accepted by her husband's family from the Welsh side.

We saw Tess a great deal and I would often drive up to see her. Soon another friend was to join the party. Brenda George who had been with me as a client since 1995 had moved from Suffolk – her former marital home - to Wiltshire and had lived near to us in Marlborough. This had been a 'return' for her after many years, since she had been born in Swindon. But now she followed us and Tess to Fishguard and bought a house not too far away.

My abiding memory of Brenda is of her standing behind the counter of '*Georgie Porgie*'. Cooking was her love and talent - as well as gardening - and she had decided to set up a cheesecake stall in the local weekly market. William helped serve on one occasion. That year we threw her a surprise birthday party, with balloons and cake, and invited one or two other close 'workshop' friends.

Fairly soon after we moved in, I started work and made regular trips by train to Mary's house for clients in London. In February I offered a five-day workshop, to take place in Tess's home. Her house was spacious, with room for three or four people to stay - depending on single or shared accommodation.

As always, the participants came from far and wide. I preferred to rely on my established client base rather than advertise locally. The title of the workshop: '*Why Tibet Works better in the West!*'

Most Tibetans are Buddhist, and during our time there we had seen many monks and several monasteries, but I felt uncomfortable in these temples. When Buddhism was brought to Tibet it overlaid the indigenous tradition, Bon: a shamanistic, animalistic religion, with a priest (gshen) or bonpo. I could feel it. It was as though a layer of 'psychic energy', lay alongside, or beneath, the beautiful spirituality of Tibet, which in some esoteric traditions is considered the heart centre of the world.

My flyer for the workshop suggested that there was a sense in which the energy in Tibet itself had become stagnant, petrified into a form no longer valid for the Spiritual Centre of the World. "Yet in our view, the true energy of Tibet remains in the wondrous air of the mountains and is a key to understanding this evolutionary moment of mankind." During those five days we explored how to understand Tibetan energy in a new and significant way.

In May, I also offered this workshop as a five-day residential in France, at the kind invitation of Barbara and Dave Smedley at their second home in the Charente in France. This was the first of several courses we held there in the next few years, attended by some of the people who over the years became a 'core group'. This time it was Elisabeth and James, Barbara's friend Val, Susan and, of course, Barbara herself.

It was easy to travel by train: Eurostar to the Gare du Nord; metro to Gare Montparnasse and train direct to Angouleme, where Dave picked us up. These workshops were the most fun. Dave, who loved to cook, went to the heights of accommodation by providing three delicious meals a day, taking in his stride the wish-list for all the complicated individual diets.

At the end of each workshop I held a theme party, and on this occasion, we held a 'heart party'.

Everyone made a gesture towards an appropriate 'costume' and Dave provided heart shaped party biscuits, as well as a gorgeous flan cake with pastry hearts on the top. I had asked the participants to 'do a turn', and I was amazed how they entered into the spirit of things. Each person did a short performance: a dance, a song, a reading, and as long as I did not have to perform myself it was great!

In June, I held two consecutive two-day weekend workshops, '*Signposts to the Future*', this time at Jan and Barrie's house in Southfields, London. They suggested again I should stay during the time they were away on their annual Greek holiday, which gave me the opportunity to work with my London clients. The participants at these workshops included 'the babies': Anna, Claire and Kelly.

William was busy too. He was asked to make a video for a local couple, to promote their Welsh tour business. He used a camera from the local e-learning centre and enjoyed the freedom of spontaneous filming for the project. At the end of the shoot, he invited Clive, a former BBC film editor living in London, to undertake the final edit.

That summer Linda came to stay from America; this time with the wish to go to Laugharne, Carmarthenshire, where Dylan Thomas settled with his wife Caitlin after their marriage. Linda, William and I did the trip and really enjoyed ourselves. We saw The Boathouse beside the Bay where the couple had lived, and looked into his writing shed, a hundred yards from the house. We visited his grave in the churchyard off the main street and had a delicious fish and chip lunch in Browns Hotel, Dylan's pub of choice.

Jan and Barrie also visited us. (Jan has always said she needs to visit each house so she can picture where we are!) And Hannah came later that month.

Hannah had now returned from Australia after five years and was living in a flat in Cromer. In September she was to spend three months in Paris, as Acting Director for the Alexander Technique Teacher Training School during the sabbatical of its original director. And a music teacher colleague who worked at a College for Performing Arts, also invited her to do some Alexander work for a course she was running, promoting the idea of physicality alongside the voice.

But this year I didn't make my annual return visit to Hannah, because in August something unforeseen and shocking happened. I discovered, via a mammogram and then biopsies at Swansea hospital, that I had DCIS (ductal carcinoma in situ). This is cancer in the milk ducts, the earliest form of breast cancer and non-invasive, but which can be so if left untreated.

My consultant at Haverford West Hospital was nice – and kind. He was not a cancer specialist, but a general surgeon, who worked closely with the cancer team in Swansea. Immediately after diagnosis I underwent an operation, but two days later his team decided I should have a second operation, to remove the surface skin, which was also affected.

A few days after that he offered me a 'preventive mastectomy and reconstruction' because he still couldn't get a boundary round the cancer cells. And suddenly I said, 'No. Stop'. I needed time to think; to take back control.

I explained I would never say never, but not now. He warned me it would come back: in two years, eight years, twenty years. "But by then you won't mind," he said, implying I would be too old to care! (It is now seventeen years later – and I can assure him I would still care!)

It was a difficult time for us both. I felt that this was the outcome of the huge shock around my mother's death and the fall-out with my brother. At that time, and almost overnight, my incredibly curly hair had gone straight, and only in the last several years has it begun to curl again. I felt that such a shock could initiate cancer.

Not long after the second operation, I went again to Barbara and Dave's in France for another five-day workshop, which coincided with their Ruby Wedding Anniversary on 20th September. No-one knew how shaken I was, but it was the best place to be: with Barbara, Elisabeth, James, Brenda, Barbara's long-time social work colleague and friend Mary Robinson – who became a regular workshop participant - and a lovely young woman, Wendy. She was new to us all, but I knew her mother Susan from workshop days with David Furlong.

I repeated the title of the London workshops: '*Signposts to the Future*', suggesting that we, as humanity, have been going around in karmic circles as a way for us to understand our history. It was time to stop the spin and step forward into a new dawn, 'into a feeling of togetherness yet separateness, in which everyone can become more of themselves. Life expands yet is contained within who and what we are'.

As before, Dave worked hard on the meals on our behalf, and went with the spirit of it all. We had established the workshop 'ritual' of an outing to a nearby village, Aubeterre, for a lovely lunch, and the end of workshop party was themed around Barbara and Dave's anniversary. Wendy and James teamed up to sing an anniversary song in the nearby chapel, and Elisabeth did a marvellous 'rock chick' impression! (James is an original member and renowned drummer of the seventies band, The Yardbirds.) There was always lots of laughter.

But after the recent stresses, William and I felt it was time to leave Fishguard. It had never felt like 'home', possibly because we sensed that the Welsh still did not welcome the English. This was confirmed when we heard the gossip around the sale of our house. We had spent a great deal of money renovating the house, and therefore felt justified in our asking price. But to the locals we were the exploitative English.

We decided to return to Marlborough. For some reason, while not quite an Anglophile, of all the counties in the UK, I like Wiltshire. In any case, this is where Emma, James and the children (by now five in number) were. They lived in Swindon Old Town, where Em was brought up, and we would be going back to an area that was familiar to us.

There is a small irony in how much I now like Swindon. In earlier days, aged twenty-four, when I worked as feature writer on *'Petticoat'*, I was given a project to travel the UK and write a comprehensive feature, comparing several key towns, including London, Newcastle, Leeds, Birmingham - and Swindon.

Somehow, I managed to offend Swindon! And when the town council complained to my editor, it was agreed I should return there to write a more favourable report. This was based on a nightclub that was hugely popular with teenagers, and fortunately I redeemed myself.

On an exploratory trip to Marlborough, one agent suggested a house she felt we might like. It was in Ramsbury, a quiet, through-street, sought-after village six miles from the town. As it turned out, the Old Bank, Ramsbury High Street was perfect.

The decommissioned bank had been converted brilliantly by a former owner - though we were attracted immediately by the original black and white tiles on the entrance hall floor. The young woman owner was in the sitting room with her brown

Labrador, in front of an open fire. The kitchen had been redesigned from the old strong room and now had an Aga. The room at the front, also with an open fire, was the old bank's reception room. What not to like?

On the day we left Fishguard in early 2004 and crossed the bridge back into England, we both felt a huge wave of relief.

CHAPTER SIX

December 2003-December 2005: Old Bank

'Bo'

Old Bank was in a row of terraced houses, along the High Street of Ramsbury. High Street suggests a far busier road than it actually was. A few people might drive through the village as the route to Marlborough but, mostly, it was only used by the locals.

We lived next door to Sue and John whose accommodation was in the former post office they used to run. John had had a stroke and his speech was quite impaired: he rode a mobility scooter. On the other side was a young couple Matt and Erica, and next to them was General John, who kindly came to the door on our arrival to proffer a bottle of milk as a welcoming present! His wife had also had a stroke.

On our first morning, Christmas Eve, we were woken by the village Silver Band playing God Rest Ye Merry Gentleman! Otherwise, on the whole, it was very quiet and we only heard the fire crew occasionally steaming past on a call-out. But we began to realise that we lived in a real English village when we went to an introductory evening for local societies. There were about fifty we could have joined in our village alone.

It became obvious that there was a hierarchy in the village. We lived on the south side, next to the river, which seemed to demarcate the 'right' bank as opposed to the 'wrong' bank! We socialised on occasion with Sheila opposite, who though slightly disabled, could often be seen lying on the ground in the church garden, doing the weeding. We had dinners with Sylvia, who sang in the choir, and her husband Edward, the local digital genius and enthusiastic member of the Silver Band.

We were also invited to occasional parties given by Jane, the real doyen of the village, and husband Michael, the respected former GP. For a short time, we attended the church as a means of joining the largest club in Ramsbury, and despite village politics, which were new to us, we really appreciated being out of Wales. There was a post office, a village shop and a bus stop.

We did not have a garden, which I found liberating. Instead, running along the side of the house was a small courtyard, where I grew plants in pots. The courtyard was fenced, but ran parallel to the footpath, leading from our side door, which was the right of way for the house just behind us.

This house was the second home of Rex and Ruth Muffett, who lived for the most part in Belsize Park, London. They introduced themselves on Christmas Day. Their proximity was mitigated by the fact they were not there often, but we were on good terms and I met Ruth socially in London from time to time. Rex had developed Alzheimers, and we had on a few occasions assisted Ruth with his care. But quite early on in our time there, he was taken ill in London and sadly died.

We really valued the various walks that were possible in and around Ramsbury. A particular favourite was to walk along the river as far as the estate of Harry Hyams of Centre Point. We heard that he entertained the founder of Ikea and the King of Sweden who stayed nearby; their favourite venue was the Red Lion pub in Axford. I would also walk the river 'block' every morning, and in winter the fields of the wetlands were full of Canada Geese.

But the best thing about Ramsbury was Bo. At last we felt we could have a cat and applied to the Newbury cat rescue. On our first visit, as we walked around the pens, only Bo showed any interest in us. So, of course, he was the one. Originally named Boris – which did not suit him at all - he was a big black cat. He was very affectionate with us, and it was only after we left several years later that we learned he was a bit of a bruiser with the other cats in the area.

In February 2004, it was William's sixtieth birthday. We had a celebration; with Emma and James and their six young children (Finn was born the year before), as well as nephews Richard and Keith, who lived in Haywards Heath, and their dad, William's brother John and sister-in-law Barbara from Warwickshire.

In May I began a series of five weekend workshops extending into October: '*Learning to Live with Abundance: exploring a new psychology*'. We looked at how we perceive ourselves when we are no longer caught in the web of past experience or reflecting who we are through the mirror of other people. Participants could attend the whole series or pick and choose. As always, they would take B & B accommodation and bring items for lunch to share.

Another advantage of Ramsbury was our closeness to the Savernake Forest. For several years running John and Barbara would rally the troops and we would have a family day there. We hired a barbecue site for the day, sometimes erect a little open marquee, and the children - and enthusiasts - would play cricket.

One of our favourite excursions was to the Ramsbury fair, with James and the boys, Toby, Ollie and Harry, who seemed to enjoy themselves. Harry went in for an egg and spoon race, while Toby, then about nine, was introduced to our friend Duncan.

His manners made us proud, although Emma confided to us later that he told her he knew he had to be very polite!

But a shock was coming. In August that year, 2004, I went on my annual visit to Myrna in Valensole. I flew to Marseille, then took the bus to Manosque, where Myrna met me.

Back at home, William had decided to find work in a nearby village pub, to keep himself busy and earn some money, and he planned to start the following day. But the day after I arrived in France, there was a phone call telling me that William had had a stroke and had been taken to Swindon hospital.

Apparently, after one stressful morning at the job, his leg had suddenly gone stiff and he felt unwell. He managed to get himself home, where Ruth persuaded him to go to the GP immediately. From there he was advised to walk home slowly while an ambulance was called.

Ruth's cleaner Sue packed his bag, and in a moment of prescience, he wrapped two potatoes he had been baking and put them in as well. He was admitted into the hospital at 5pm and parked in the only available space – a storeroom with a bed. The serving of food had finished, so the baked potatoes were a Godsend!

I moved heaven and earth to get a flight from Marseille the following day and the journey seemed endless. But I got to the hospital by 3pm that afternoon. John and Barbara had been in the morning, and Emma was with him when I arrived. The following morning, he was sent for tests and x-rays. And a day later sent home.

William had no idea what had happened to him. He had no awareness of stroke at all. He had a stiff leg, a limp, and no energy. For three days he stayed in bed while Bo lay across his legs, and it was clear that he only left William's side – apart from his nightly prowls - when he felt he had done his work.

(In fact, Bo's healing talents were in evidence again when sometime later my auntie Eileen came to stay. She had painful shingles and while William offered her healing, Bo lay along the top of the chair and against her neck and back. When the shingles actually improved the following day, she was convinced it was Bo's magic - William wasn't given a mention!)

William contacted the Red Cross, which provided temporary walking sticks, and found that the local representative was Jane. He felt fragile and limited in ability, so walking was important. Each day he could do a few yards more. A fortnight later he was called to the Geriatric Unit (at age sixty!) to be given blood pressure pills.

In fact, it has taken years for William to find a good combination of pills without incapacitating side effects, and only now has this search settled into something relatively benign. William slowly improved, but we now described ourselves as living on 'stroke row' with our closest neighbours in that category too!

The work I do is difficult to explain, even now, which is why I have always preferred to be recommended by word of mouth. I rarely talk about it to the people around me, and in all our moves, as far as neighbours have been concerned, William and I are retired. But for the first time, I decided to advertise my work locally.

I posted a flyer in the post office offering a short series of guided meditation evenings at Old Bank, which attracted a group of six – a nice number. Although a little shocked at the personal nature of the meditations, they seemed to enjoy the experience, and one or two then came as private clients.

One of these was Erica, who lived in Marlborough. She practised a therapy called Human Design, and I had an interesting session of her work. My 'design' was 'Manifester', which did indicate that what I did was 'pioneering'. She suggested that one thing people with my design needed was a long time to 'wind-down' after the day, which finally gave me permission – and an excuse - for going to bed as early as I do! It has seemed strange to other people, but a three hour wind-down, reading, listening to the radio, suits me fine!

One of the best things that happened in Ramsbury was finding Rachel, a practitioner of Shiatsu. Seventeen years on, she is still my 'healer of choice'. Rachel lived in Woodborough, where her family owned a large area of the land. Following a divorce, she lived with her parents, practising in a room at the front of the house. Later she bought her own house in the village, but still worked in the family home.

I had learned early on to be wary of who I let work on my body. In our 'hands-on' practising at the College of Healing in the eighties, I had experienced that not everyone is 'clear' and can often put their own unconscious 'stuff' into the mix when doing their practice. The only male participant who felt clear to me was Barrie, a homeopath, who I later consulted, and has been a friend ever since.

After my cancer scare, I wanted to find someone 'clear', and immediately I liked Rachel. Shiatsu, is a Japanese practice, involving finger pressure on acupressure points. I trusted her ability to sense what was happening in my body, because I could feel it for myself as she worked to release and relieve.

Rachel had been recommended to me by Nadia, who was now a strong feature in our life in Ramsbury. I had met Nadia at Le Plan in the mid-eighties, and in recent years she had attended my workshops. She had now moved from London to Froxfield, a village not far from us, into a small apartment on the Duchess of Devonshire estate - the old Alms Houses. She was now near her daughter Nicky in Woodborough, who was a friend of Rachel. Hence the connection.

Tess had moved from Fishguard too, knowing that Fran and Derek would not be joining her there after all. She had bought a house back in Abingdon, and so we three, Nadia, Tess and I, the Le Plan alumni, were within distance for renewed friendship. When with Tess, we often saw Fran and Derek and the children, particularly now they had moved to Long Wittenham. Brenda, in the meantime, had moved from Fishguard to Aberdeen to be near her son.

Despite his stroke, William was happy for me to continue my programme and in September I held another five-day workshop *'The Way to Happiness'*, at Dave and Barbara's home in the Charente. The regulars: Brenda, Susan, Mary and Elisabeth were there, and I remember particularly an exercise on the significance of the Spleen in relation the Life Force..

In January 2005, I began a series of monthly Sunday workshops, to run throughout the year *'Twelve Days of the New Creation'*. I proposed that after four years of leading groups and clients towards a 'new era', this, the year of the Rooster, would - to quote *Chinese Heritage* - 'herald the dawn after the long night', and we would experience change, internally and externally.' I wanted now to offer teaching rather than a therapeutic programme. Still experiential, it would be an information year.

In April 2005, we were the invited guests, with Barbara and Dave, to Elisabeth and James' wedding in Roussillon. They had moved to the Vaucluse from Herne Hill, in part thanks to the guidance. In answer to a question, the guides had suggested they look for a place in France with a 'yellow ochre' landscape, and it was Myrna who told us that Roussillon fitted the description perfectly.

We went by train to Avignon where James met us and took us to our hotel. The day itself was a delight. The four of us walked to the Mayor's parlour - Barbara and I carrying huge bouquets of cherry blossom (Elisabeth's favourite) - and met the couple there.

The Mayor, wearing his outstanding mayoral sash, carried out the civil ceremony, and then Dave drove all of us to the reception for an extended lunch. Rather than traditional speeches Elisabeth asked each of us to say something appropriate to the occasion - which for my part included a channelling. The sun shone on a perfect day.

In June we were back to Barbara and Dave's in France for another five-day workshop *'Playing in the Light'*: 'to explore how the nature of Light itself was changing; as it trickles into the body and mind of each individual'.

In July it was my sixtieth birthday. Emma, James and the children came to Old Bank, as well as the Davisons in full measure, which was kind. Later that summer, Tass and David and daughter Kathy spent a long weekend at the Warner Leisure Centre at Littlecote House, not far from Ramsbury.

We had often walked across the fields and had a cup of tea there, but on this occasion, they invited us for a sumptuous evening meal. In fact, Littlecote had originally been Jo's family home, and two or three years before she had taken me round on a short tour of reminiscence.

The saddest thing that year was the death of Tess. It came so suddenly; the news that she had lung cancer. There were times it was clear she was short of breath, but it was a shock to know the truth. I remember my last visit to Abingdon where I prepared a lunch of salmon. As always, we did some guidance work: Tess was the most ardent supporter of the work.

A few days later she died, and we attended her funeral near Oxford officiated by her former husband Rob. I was asked to do the eulogy, and I remembered my dearest friend Tess. She was strong, determined, committed, with a huge capacity for friendship: each of us felt we were special to her. Other people spoke, but the most outstanding memory as we left the church, was the music: Bob Marley's *'Be Happy'*, which made us all smile. She never forgot her time with Rob in Jamaica, when her children, Fran and Hugh, were young.

Lorna St Aubyn also died in 2005. We had lost touch by then, but I knew she had had a stroke, and was totally paralysed, except for movement of her eyelids. Lorna had featured – quite cruelly – in her son Edward St Aubyn's semi-autobiographical *'Patrick Melrose'* novels, and after her death she was portrayed again in *'At Last'* the fifth and final book of the series. More recently the novels became a five-part television drama series starring Benedict Cumberbatch.

Later that year I visited Hannah. She had left Cromer and moved into a cottage on Lord Buxton's estate in Stiffkey and become friendly with his wife and family. Aubrey Buxton was the founder of Anglia television, and he initiated and presented *'Survival'*, one of television's longest and most successful nature documentary series. It ran for forty years. His daughter Cindy was a presenter, environmentalist and wild-life film-maker who also worked mainly on *'Survival'*.

Once a month I would meet my friend Barrie, the homeopath, in Marlborough, as I had done when we lived at High View several years before. He came to visit his aunt who had once been a Dame, or House Mistress, at Marlborough College, but was now in poor health. We would drink coffee in the café of the deconsecrated church, now used as a culture venue.

For William things had improved. Although his leg has always been slightly comprised, he had become bored with fragility. He decided to email Handicap International in China, now headed by a young Belgian, Koen Sevenants, volunteering to make videos for them. Koen replied that, as it happened, they had just bought a new camera and there was an enthusiastic young man in the office, Forest, who was happy to be a trainee.

William was invited to Beijing on an expenses-only basis and in August 2005, set off immediately for an initial six weeks to do a recce, staying in an HI apartment. Koen had put forward a proposal to the UK Department for International Development and, as a result, had been awarded a million pound grant to 'do something for disabled people' - particularly in Yuexi, a very poor area where disabled people were not supported.

The team; Forest, Frank - assistant director of HI - the interpreter and William, flew to Chengdu, followed by short trip in a propellor plane, then a taxi, a train and another taxi to this remote county in the southern province of Sechuan.

On their last morning, they decided to film an extra segment; of an elderly man living in a 'hovel' and looked after by his wife. Filming took place on a narrow pathway beside a sewage stream, so when a bicycle came straight towards William, he stepped to one side. His foot slipped and he fell into the water.

He hurt his shoulder badly, and the pain was excruciating. Eventually the interpreter put him in a bicycle rickshaw to return to the hotel - and cuddled him for comfort! Later that day he was taken to a poor and rather grubby hospital for a shoulder x-ray, which confirmed he had torn a shoulder muscle. The following day, William took the circuitous journey back to Beijing, accompanied by Frank who was delegated to look after him.

The shoulder was a problem for several months, but William came home soon after the incident to prepare for a longer trip, and the most exciting prospect of our time in Ramsbury. We were to spend six months in China.

In preparation for the trip our first concern was Bo. We knew that William's daughter Mel and husband Steve were in transition, and suggested they take over the house while we were away. They loved Bo and were happy to live in Ramsbury, so it worked perfectly.

Our relationship with Mel has always been problematic. We explained it to ourselves that as the youngest she had always taken on responsibility for the family - especially when William and his former wife Christine parted. At that time, Emma was twelve and Mel eleven, and she did once agree that it had weighed too heavily on her.

Mel is a charismatic woman and people are drawn to her instinctively. But then, it seems, the responsibility for such closeness becomes too much, and she needs to escape. Whenever this happened Steve was, and is, a stalwart, supportive and loyal figure by her side. Of course, over the years we understood – and experienced – that there was a lot of 'blame' on the parents for her perceived predicament.

In fact, I had only recently met Mel for the first time. For the eleven years since William and I got together, there had been an estrangement. I was yet to encounter – and then endure – the vagaries of Mel's behaviour, and the 'puppet on a string' years of being 'in or out' of her favour. As, we learned eventually, did Emma and James, the children and her own mother. But for now, this first come-back in our relationship was warm and for a few years she felt like a friend. It was a relief for William to have his daughter back.

Armed with a six month supply of blood pressure pills, William left for Beijing in early September and stayed once again in the Handicap International apartment. His first project, with Forest, was to film an HI supported nursery in Nanning. They took a sleeper train from Beijing at 3pm one afternoon and arrived twenty-six hours later, at 5pm the following day. This long journey gave him the perfect opportunity to witness the vast changes in landscape throughout China.

In the meantime, I was getting ready to leave. But just before I did so, I learned that Nadia was in hospital with a clot on the brain, and I went to see her immediately. I felt bad to be leaving her just then, but with a little cheer to her improvement, she promised to email me each week with the results of '*Strictly Come Dancing*'!

CHAPTER SEVEN

December 2005-July 2006: Tuanjaihu

'Six months in Beijing'

On Koen's advice we found a three-bedroom flat, on the eleventh floor, in Tuanjaihu Residential District, in the same block as the HI apartment. It was in the eastern part of the city off the Fifth Ring Road. It came with beds but nothing more, but to William's amazement, within three days I had it completely furnished.

We discovered that if we got in a taxi and said 'Yi jia jia Ju', in half an hour we would be set down outside Ikea! I had a field day there, which of course included lunch. The Chinese version of an Ikea menu was slightly different, but they still served the ubiquitous meat balls. Along a side road from Tuanjaihu we had found a curtain shop and a day later curtains were delivered and fitted. Then a man arrived with plants on a bike, and we were done!

It was a nice apartment, though we were often woken by high heels clattering across the wooden floor of the apartment above us, and on Saturdays by her playing the piano. We had a view across the skyline and became hyper aware of the awful yellow, polluting smog.

Part of the rental included a flat screen television. The Chinese were not allowed to own a satellite dish, but they cast a blind eye over foreigners who chose to do so. We could see one or two from our apartment and had some fun when a cloak and dagger team of four men – recommended to us - arrived to install a dish and receiver, which they had hidden in a blanket.

Thank goodness for satellite, as a relief from China Television news in English, and '*Barnaby*' (*Midsomer Murders*) with Chinese subtitles. We could watch BBC world news and films and realised that access to our own language and culture was important - which is probably why we gravitated with such pleasure to Xin Ba Ke (Starbucks!). This was the only place you could get coffee and buns for breakfast! The taxi to get there cost ten yuan (£1).

We spent a lot of time in Starbucks, usually arriving at 7am. It was directly opposite the Diplomatic Compound where HI had their office, so William did not have far to go for work. One particular man was always working there, on his computer at a corner table. When we finally spoke to him, he told us he was a freelance journalist for American publications. It was advanced for the time to use Starbucks as an office!

One Sunday morning a man came hurtling into the coffee shop and made straight for us. He begged for money 'because he had lost his wallet', but we said no and turned away. The following Sunday the same man rushed in and came up to us, with the same request! William told him, 'No. The same as last week'!

William chose to take taxis, but I preferred the bus - or the metro, which ran in what felt like huge caverns. It was here, while waiting for trains, that Chinese young people would come up to me and ask to speak in English. It was an opportunity they were not embarrassed to take.

I found an internet café near Tiananmen Square, and went there often. For two weeks I got the *Strictly* results from Nadia, but the following week there was nothing, which got me worried.

I emailed Mel, asking if she would phone Nadia's daughter Nicky.

To my horror when she emailed back, she told me that Nadia had died. Sent home from the hospital, Nicky had later found her in her cottage, two days after she had died from a brain haemorrhage. Of course, I was really sad not to be able to go to the funeral, and asked Mel if she would organise flowers. Tess had been seventy-two, Nadia sixty-six. To have lost two close friends in so short a time was devastating.

Just before Christmas, while William was busy, I decided to visit Kunming, another 'must do' in China. I flew to spend a few days in this capital of the southern Yunnan Province, in the west, where my modern hotel played a constant loop of western Christmas music. I explored mostly on foot, walking the length of the main street looking at everything along the way, but I did take a bus to the famous and fabulous Kunming flower market.

I also took a coach tour to the UNESCO-listed Stone Forest and walked amongst the unique limestone formation of rocks in this spectacular natural attraction. On our way back we stopped for lunch and were provided with a local Sechuan dish. When the tour guide realised it was just too hot for me to eat, he was kind enough to ask for an alternative. I returned to Beijing just in time for Christmas.

The Chinese do celebrate Christmas in a certain way, despite it being such a different culture. The shops are decorated, and you hear Christmas music everywhere. I bought some tree lights at the Friendship Store which sells gifts and speciality goods - predominantly for tourists and the diplomatic community. On an earlier visit, I had bought my down-filled 'China Coat' from there - which I still wear!

We noticed, as we walked around this particular area, that there were many young western couples with Chinese babies in prams and pushchairs. In those days, with the one-child policy and a family's preferred wish to have a boy, there were many arranged adoptions of girls. In fact, Koen and his wife had done so.

Christmas day was a normal day for the locals, but for HI it was a holiday. Around the corner from Starbucks, at the back of the block, was an American diner run by a Canadian national married to a Chinese woman. It was a favourite venue for William, and we decided to book there for our not quite Christmasy lunch – though we did have Christmas pudding and custard!

Around 4pm we took a taxi to a tea house in a narrow lane near a hutong. We had been invited by Lizi Hesling for tea with a small group of her friends. I had stayed in touch with Lizi since 1997, when Paz and I had come to study Mandarin at the Capital Normal University.

Lizi now lived in a hutong, a traditional courtyard compound with several dwellings and a communal squat toilet in one corner. It was very basic, and she loved living there, but soon all the hutongs would be demolished in the continuing modernisation of Beijing.

We reflect on that Christmas day tea as one of the most bizarre we have known. We were old enough to be the parents of these young people, but they made us feel very welcome. We knew Lizi was gay and looked forward to meeting her new partner Da Jun, a film editor. There were two other young gay women present - and most memorably - Kitz, who was our first encounter – in 2006 – with a transgender man.

Kitz was also a film editor, and he and William spent time talking about film-making. But the strange thing is that Kitz and I have been in touch by email ever since that one meeting on that one afternoon. I have followed his journeying back and forth from his home in Kuala Lumpur and his favoured place of work Beijing.

I have heard the vagaries of his life as a transgender person; as a man trying to get a film project off the ground, and also needing work. I did a couple of sessions for him in the following years, and he recommended one or two friends who would consult via FaceTime.

At that time Lizi was doing translating work for the English language channel at Central China Television, and later did news voice-overs. In fact, during our visit she kindly agreed to record a voice-over for Koen's own charity, Morning Tears, which supported the children of parents who had been executed or had long-term prison sentences, and for which William had made a video.

In later years Lizi and DaJun had a child, Ouwen, born to Lizi by a Chinese donor. Eventually they went for a civil partnership in the UK, but a few years later separated permanently and Lizi returned to England with Ouwen. She is now a freelance film and video editor in London.

William and I managed to live on HI expenses of thirteen dollars a day. The aim of his time in Beijing was to oversee Forest in the making of HI promotional videos on childcare. They worked closely with Karen, a German member of staff and newly qualified physiotherapist.

Over the time, Forest gave William a complete run-down of life in China, and he thoroughly enjoyed being part of a small working team. In fact, he feels on balance that he gained more from Forest than he offered.

I had found another Mandarin course, not too far from Tuanjiehu. I would wait at the bus stop every morning in minus five degree weather (for which I had acquired some long johns) and take the few stops north to school. Once I left the bus it was a short walk, past the smart Kempinski Lufthansa hotel where the airline crews would stay during their stopovers. During our whole time in Beijing it was '*hen leng*' (very cold!)

The students were mostly like me, not youngsters, but older foreign nationals in the city. I made particular friends with Bita, an Iranian girl. Her family had fled from Iran to the UK in 1979 after a crackdown on their Bahai faith. The family home was in Brighton, but she and her husband had come to Beijing with their delightful eight year old daughter to set up an Iranian restaurant. We went there several times.

Bita knew I was engaged in a different kind of spirituality, and on one occasion invited me to a Bahai meeting. I felt I couldn't refuse, but although the Bahia believe in the essential truth of all religions, it was just too formulaic for me, so I didn't go again.

On one occasion we did go to Church. William had been to a Mac computer conference, and the church - which was forbidden to Chinese nationals - was recommended by a fellow participant. The service took place in a former cinema which held two thousand people, and we had to show our passports to prove our nationality. It was a 'happy-clappy' kind of event with the words of the hymns projected on the screen. It was certainly an experience.

The biggest festival in China is New Year, and on an ice-cold day in February we walked in thick snow to the Celebration Park. As we joined the path, maybe five meters wide, there was what can only be described as a throng: more people than we had ever seen in one place before. There were flags and streamers and tableaux, and horse drawn sleds.

Walking across the canal bridge the river below was frozen. Everyone was making for the fairground. I tried my hand at one stall - where you threw balls at a target – and to my astonishment I won! The stallholder walked along the line of gifts on offer, and at the end he picked the ugliest toy he could find: a large Winnie the Pooh Piglet. We became quite fond of Piglet, who we re-named Uglet.

Another iconic Beijing site is the Silk Market, which was around the corner from William's office. We went there several times and got used to the necessary haggling that was part of the experience. We were told to start at one-third of the asking price, and then haggle.

We left Beijing with one or two fashion label garments, like Polo blouses and Ralph Lauren shirts. William's prize possession was a winter jacket. We were never quite sure if any of it was legal, but as we understood it, items were ordered from Chinese factories with the assumption that a few left the premises.

Another uncertainty was the legality of the DVD sellers. Young men would walk along the streets, mainly around the diplomatic area, trying to sell their wares - the latest western films. We did buy one once, and realised the films were copied from the screen in the cinema! Definitely not legal!

To William's delight and surprise, a few months into our time in Beijing, Sheila Purves, director of the WHO Collaboration Centre for Rehabilitation in Hong Kong, asked Koen if she could use him and the HI equipment to make a film about their work - for WHO Hong Kong. William had met Sheila on her several visits to the office and had filmed a talk she gave for HI.

We flew to Hong Kong, and stayed in Sheila's headquarters, a hospital overlooking the sea, where we could watch the vast containerships moving across our view. The assignment took a week to film, with William doing the camera work, but we also had time to explore the tourist sites.

We walked in Victoria Park, where we were fascinated to see several parties of brides posing for wedding photos in their beautiful gowns. We took the funicular to the Peak and strolled around the perimeter for the famous views. We boarded a ferry to Macao and spent time on the beach there.

But while we were in Hong Kong, William got a fax from Koen, saying HI could no longer afford to pay him expenses. There had already been murmurs, but finally it was clear that even thirteen dollars a day, over these months, was going beyond a tight budget. William did feel a little miffed, considering he was working for nothing, but despite that he went back to the HI office to edit Sheila's film.

I didn't go straight back to Beijing. A couple of weeks before we left for Hong Kong, Mary had come to stay for a day or two. As an experienced traveller she was planning a China trip on her own but came to us on the way. She and I decided that as I would be in Hong Kong we could meet in Guilin, Guanxi, which both of us had dreamed of seeing.

Guilin is the dramatic landscape of limestone karst hills often depicted in advertisements about China. At the centre are two lakes: Shanhu (cedar) and Ronghu (banyan) which remain from a medieval moat that ran around the city. I went by train from Hong Kong, changing at Shenzhen in Guangzhou. Mary came from Kunming.

In our short time there we took a boat trip up the Li River to Yangshuo, where we saw the iconic sight of a man fishing with a cormorant. We stayed overnight and then, back in Guilin, we took a tour to the Reed Flute cave, with its huge stalagmites and stalactites, spectacularly illuminated by coloured lighting. We then flew back to Beijing, from where, after another couple of days, Mary took a plane back London.

Not long after our return, the secretary in the HI office said she had a friend who needed English voices for course material for students in banking, and would we take part. We agreed and went to their college for a morning's work. We sat on a sofa in front of the microphone, while two or three staff stood behind the recording equipment to supervise.

As soon as we recorded our first conversation – between a bank teller and a customer - they looked at each other, smiled and nodded, so we knew our English had passed muster! We were honoured to do it and our reward was a magnificent lunch and a small cash payment.

In March 2007, Elisabeth and James came to Beijing for a six-day pilgrimage to the Tibetan monasteries in Yunnan, and I had applied to go with them. Several years before, James had become a student of Buddhism and the teachings of His Holiness the head of the Drukpa Lineage. A Buddhist retreat in Henley had first captured his imagination, and he had introduced his enthusiasm to Elisabeth. They both attended talks in London.

For me, I confess, it was more the opportunity to see the famous sacred mountain monasteries, which otherwise I would not be able to do. Elisabeth and James came to stay for a few days before the three of us flew to Kunming to join the sixty or so other pilgrims.

Our tour – in three coaches – began in Dali, a big, open, spacious city. But our destination was Jizushan – Chicken Foot Mountain – one of the famous Buddhist mountains in Binchuan County, Yunnan. It was three hundred and seventy kilometers west of Kunming, and at its summit was Jinding Temple.

Unfortunately, James had arrived in Beijing suffering the after-effects of pneumonia and still felt unwell. He decided to remain in the hotel, while Elisabeth and I joined the group on the incredible mountain ascent. Enthusiasts do hike or take mules, but we began in the cable car, and then climbed the steep slope to the summit. It was here I became more clearly aware of His Holiness and a companion lama.

Our overnight stay is one never to be forgotten! Housed in dormitory bedrooms, men and women together, I was amongst strangers and felt uneasy. Fortunately, since James' bed was spare, I could change rooms to be with Elisabeth, and yet more strangers!

It was a long night and the 'facilities' in the morning were even more unnerving. In a large room with a porcelain channel all round, men and women squatted in public to do their business. Presumably a large wash of water would eventually clear the debris! Fortunately, all the women felt uncomfortable and agreed to 'watch the door' in turn while we segregated the arrangements.

That morning James decided to follow us. He took a horse and then the cable car but was amused to see us in the pods coming down as he was going up. To his disappointment, he had missed the glorious and famous sunrise from the peak.

Our next stop was Lijiang, home to the Naxi and other ethnic minority groups who made up fifty-five percent of the population there. We strolled around amongst these vibrant and colourful people, before moving on to Shangrila and the amazing Ganden Sumtsenling Monastery.

There were many steps to the top, and stunning views, and way below us we saw a Buddhist funeral. Hawks were soaring in the cloudless blue sky, waiting their chance to attack the body which would be left to their devices.

On the last evening of the pilgrimage, which was His Holiness' birthday, there was a celebration dinner. Sitting at the top table, His Holiness spoke of the pilgrimage, and then at the end of the meal invited people up for an individual blessing. I –

and perhaps one other person – didn't go. It didn't feel right for me to do so.

James and Elisabeth stayed with us for another night or two and then flew back to London. William and I left in July. Despite the hundreds of flights I had taken and the huge amount of travelling I had done in my life, particularly in the seventies and eighties, I had always been terrified of flying. From the moment of take-off until the wheels touched the ground on landing, I was fearful.

So when we landed at Heathrow, I finally made up my mind. I need never take another plane again!

CHAPTER EIGHT

July 2006-October 2007: Old Bank and Kew

'Fulfilling a dream'

When we returned, Mel and Steve had organised the rental of a cottage in Winterbourne Monkton, two or three miles from Marlborough. During our time away, they had fallen in love with Bo and, somehow, it was agreed he should move on with them. We missed him a lot.

I did one weekend workshop soon after we returned, and then in January 2007 I began a course of four Sunday workshops *'New Skills for Old'*, to be held at Jo's health centre in Broadway Market, Bethnal Green. She had opened the centre in 1996, and it was the perfect opportunity to work with the London clientele and some new clients.

In January and March, I also ran a two-weekend course under the same title in Ramsbury. We would look at the rapid pace of technology and some of the ethical dilemmas it posed. We would speak about the dire future of the environment, and how old skills might not be up to the task of tackling these issues.

The idea of these weekends was to explore our 'visionary apparatus' in whichever way was unique for each individual and how to take ourselves seriously in this fast moving world at an incredible moment of change: the experience of being human in a far bigger way; and opening up to our immense creative potential.

I also continued my monthly trips to London to work at Mary's. I went by train from Hungerford station, where it was easy to park. William and I went to Hungerford regularly. There was Bo's old vet, a garden centre and a health food shop, but most important, a favourite coffee house, where we were such regular customers that on one occasion, we were invited to a charity evening which William attended.

Quietly drinking his tea at the event - William is teetotal - he was embarrassed to find himself standing right in front of Lord Carnarvon who had just been introduced as the evening's speaker. Lord Carnarvon's stately home famously became the location for Lord Grantham in Downton Abbey.

Already by January we were hovering on the idea of another move. I had fallen out of love with the limitations of Ramsbury, feeling I was 'too young' to need a post office, a bus stop and a local village shop. What I meant by that is I did not want to feel retired – not yet.

One afternoon I was 'googling' the idea of a flat in Normandy to rent for a month, and one click led to another! By chance I touched on a house for sale, six miles from Villedieu-les-Poeles, in La Manche, and no more was needed to spur me on!

I told William I would just pop up to the Ramsbury estate agent to get his view on the value of our house. Though his last words as I went out of the door were 'don't bring the agent back', fifteen minutes later I was back with the man!

That was on a Thursday, and by Monday we were in Normandy, viewing Le Perrey in the village of Beslon! We had taken the ferry from Portsmouth to Caen the previous day and stayed overnight night at a B & B near Lessay, a little further north on the Cotentin peninsular. I had seen this was also for sale, but despite the fabulous stew we were given for supper, we knew it was not for us.

We drove to Beslon the following morning. It was 20th January and snowing. Maurice, one of the owners, met us at the metal gates to the drive. He showed us into the first building, a separate gite. And then took us to the main house, where he introduced us to his partner Roy, who made us a cup of tea.

Maurice and Roy showed us round their home, a typical Normandy longhouse. They explained that they had decided to split their land in half and were building a new house on the other side. Either property could be for sale, and they would live next door.

We knew the only option for us would be the old house, and Maurice continued our tour around the five acre property. Apart from the gite, this included a walled vegetable garden, a few outbuildings and a wild patch on the perimeter with a low stream running through.

Just as we were walking back across one of the fields a 'wild' white horse called Aurore suddenly came hurtling straight towards me. My reaction was to run, and I was relieved to make the gate ahead of her! (We learned later that even Maurice was more than a little scared of Aurore.)

We drove back to the tarmac road and took a short detour through the village of Beslon, on our way to Villedieu-les-Poeles. We stayed the night in the St Pierre, a traditional hotel in the main street, which became a favourite.

The following day, we walked up the road to the Samovar tea rooms, which offered internet connection, and where, by chance, we met Geoff and Pauline. They turned out to be expats from Newcastle. Geoff was using his own Mac computer, and that led us to a Mac conversation.

We had made up our minds. As surprising as it was to think of living in France, we were excited at the prospect. Le Perrey had been a cold house – with only the use of paraffin heaters and a wood burner, so we would need to install central heating. But this was the house for us.

On our return to Rambury we put our house - which was sale ready - on the market. We had added the finishing touches that we knew we liked ourselves. We had cleared the loft space and ordered a new name plate for Old Bank. Two days later – to the estate agent's surprise - the house was sold, and a fortnight later we were back in France for a second viewing of Le Perrey.

We learned later that other people who had landed in the area had probably been searching for years, travelling all over France. I loved France as I had lived in Provence in the eighties, but I knew the climate there was too hot for me. Normandy was perfect.

Without wanting to look any further, we made an offer on the property which was accepted. We celebrated by inviting Maurice and Roy to lunch at the Union, the café of their choice in Villedieu. It all felt like serendipity - as it did when we met Geoff and Pauline again, in the bank. They would become two in a circle of really nice friends.

Although Roy had wanted to stay in their original home, they agreed to move to the new house, which was not yet finished. They guessed it would be another six months before it was fully habitable, which gave us the opportunity to do something we had both dreamed of doing at some point in our lives. We decided to take a six-month rental in Kew, an expensive area of London where neither of us could have afforded to buy.

After one or two false starts we found a three bedroom flat in Grosvenor Court, a gated block right opposite Kew Gardens. And in April 2007 we moved, with all our furniture:

some to furnish the apartment and the rest to store in a spare room. The valiant removal men took it all up four flights of stairs!

We loved Kew. The May trees were beginning to blossom in the gardens, and spring was in the air. William's first excursion, on 7th April, was to walk along the towpath to watch the boat race. Our only concern was the noise of the planes that flew virtually above our heads to and from Heathrow. Flights began around 5am and ended towards midnight, but the agent had suggested that after a while you tuned out the sound. Amazingly she was right.

Soon after we arrived, the doorbell rang. When I opened the door, a beautiful Adonis – not unlike Jonty Kelt in Shanghai - announced himself as Zac Goldsmith, our local candidate. I was so flustered, I could only tell him we were not local, politely say thank you for calling, and closed the door!

There were so many simple pleasures - like early morning breakfast at Starbucks near Kew Station. When Elisabeth and James came to Kew, staying in the Coach and Horses Hotel as they did quite often, their favourite destination was the wholefood shop Olivers. And Elisabeth and I would meet for lunch or coffee at the famous Maids of Honour tearooms.

We bought a season ticket to Kew Gardens and spent a lot of time there. We also acquired our first 'senior citizens' bus passes! This made a huge and helpful difference to travel around London, whether by bus or tube. It was an easy journey to work at Mary's house in Bloomsbury, while William's pleasure was walking to the National Archives in Kew to do some research.

Richmond was a favourite destination on the bus, not least for the cinema. On one occasion when William went to Richmond for a cup tea, he saw actor Peter Bowles buying a newspaper. A few steps later he saw Richard E. Grant. (It is that kind of place.) He says he was wondering who the third star would be, and as he turned the corner, he saw…me! He's a good man!

I was now living very near Maria Saekel Jelkman. I had been introduced to Maria by Wendy, a participant at the workshop I held at Barbara and Dave's in France, immediately after my cancer operations in 2004. Maria was a completely unique homeopath, with her own – possibly eccentric - way of divining things and her own formulas for remedies.

She had devised her system after curing herself of cancer as a younger woman (she was now in her mid-late eighties) and in fact we all went to see her in the end. At that time, because of the cancer, I was happy to accept her diagnoses and take the remedies, and to follow the particular recommendations on what might be taken from or added to my diet.

After the first batch of remedies I settled down with just two that felt appropriate to me and I have taken them every day since. But Maria obviously assumed that my being in Kew was a 'sign' that I should study her work and make it my own. I agreed to do a short course of training with her – because I did not like to say no, and she was a strongly persuasive woman!

I went to her home for several mornings and was made to practise using the pendulum to divine the 'rates' for the remedies. This made me uncomfortable, since my own guidance already precluded these methods now, and I didn't quite trust my own accuracy. For lunch she gave me sandwiches made from items that were strictly against her recommended diet, and which I would not normally choose to eat. It felt at odds.

After a few days, feeling more and more like a fish out of water, I finally told her that though I valued her work hugely, it was not for me to take on: I felt I had my own work to do. After that, I was reluctant to go back to Maria. I knew that Wendy's mother Susan, a homeopath herself, had trained with Maria, so I asked her if she would provide the pills for me. She has done so willingly and consistently ever since.

Kew was a marvellous central destination for visitors to come and see us. Sophia and Jeremy were living in Hampton - just before they moved to Berkhamsted - and therefore not so far away from us. My cousin Chris and husband John came from Dorset, and William's nephew and godson Richard came from Buckingham Palace. As a surveyor, he was part of the team that looked after the royal buildings.

One of the highlights of my time in Kew was the invitation to a reunion of *'Fab-208'* people, nearly forty years on! Originally called *'Fabulous'* before a tie-up with Radio Luxembourg, we were to celebrate Editor Betty Hale's eightieth birthday. The hostess was Annie Moore, who in my time on the young IPC magazine – devoted to pop music and celebrities - was picture editor.

Betty, who was a particular friend of Annie's, had been assistant editor in my time, but became editor after Unity Hall left to become Woman's Editor for *'The News of the World'*. She and Annie had worked together since *'Fab'* days.

It was incredible to see people after all this time, especially from my era. Heather Kirby, fashion editor, and Sally - who I still meet - who was then her assistant. June Southworth, a fellow feature writer who went on to the *'Daily Mail'*. Shirley Smith, picture editor before Annie, who went to the *'Sunday Times'*. Peter Pugh Cook, the photographer I had worked with on many stories, and at one time Annie's husband.

There were other women from later times and Keith Altham, well-known PR man for the biggest names in rock, back in the day. (Sadly Annie, who was by then a member of BAFTA, died in 2014. Sally and I met later that year for lunch in the Maids of Honour, Kew, to celebrate our long *Fab* friendship.)

In June I held four one-day weekend workshops in the apartment: '*Allowing Yourself to be Exceptional*', with the choice to take all four or each individually. The workshops would be on the same theme; but different according to the needs of those who were there - touching into the heights of their awareness.

That year seventh grandchild Martha was born. And on one occasion William went to Paddington to meet granddaughter Lauren who was travelling up from Swindon for an audition. Lauren's trajectory in life was to be an actress. She had danced and acted since a child and at this point, at the age of thirteen, was about to go to Sylvia Young's Stage School. She had already appeared as a dancer in the West End show '*Billy Elliott*', and as Bonnie Langford's daughter in '*Hotel Babylon*' on television.

William loved being present for the auditioning process, making him feel younger and 'down with the kids'! Though when the casting director, in passing comment on Lauren's performance, said 'she was very good grandad', reality kicked in!

In September, just before we left for France, we attended the wedding of William's niece Sarah, a nurse, to J-P. J-P is French and works as a scientist at DEFRA. The wedding took place in the Forest of Dean, where her brother Christopher lived. Eventually her parents, William's brother Mike and his wife Margaret would also move there - from Perth in Scotland. Sarah asked William to read a lesson.

We moved to France in October 2007, although William left several days before me, with his car jam-packed with our belongings. I stayed to organise the removals and was scheduled to arrive a few days after he reached Le Perrey. William remembers how exciting it was. He had always wanted to live in France, but says it was the comfort of knowing I had done it before that made it possible.

It was arranged that William would stay in the gite which Maurice and Roy had left furnished. Early the following morning he was woken by their Basset Hound, Cybele, who was barking non-stop outside the door. At that moment William decided he had to make friends with her, and Cybele became a regular feature in our lives.

After two or three days I drove to the ferry. Another dream was about to come true.

CHAPTER NINE

October 2007-December 2008: Le Perrey 1

'Space to breathe'

Le Perrey was the name of the four-house Hamlet at the end of a mile-long lane, and another mile from the tiny village of Beslon. Maurice and Roy – and Cybele - were now next door, with their five rescue horses and several sheep. Richard and Barbara had the house beyond them – and we were all English ex-pats. A little further along was Michel – and later a girlfriend - the only French nationals.

All of this land was once owned by Monsieur and Madame Binet, now an elderly couple who lived a little above and beyond us, off the main road to Villedieu. Madame Binet still leased the huge field next to us to a local farmer, Christoff, who for the most part grew maize for cattle feed. At one point we thought to negotiate for that land but decided against it. We reflected that the boundary was distanced enough.

I am a self-confessed Francophile. I have lived in French-speaking countries (France and Switzerland) for nineteen years of my life, and of all the houses, Le Perrey was, and is, my favourite. So much more space was possible at Normandy prices than anything we could afford at home, with a little bit to spare for the many changes we wanted to make. We just loved it there.

Unfortunately, on our first step into the house we discovered a serious problem: a leak in the downstairs cloakroom. Clearly, we needed a plumber *tout de suite*. Luckily Robine, a local enterprise in Villedieu, could send a man straight away, who eventually delivered the irritating news.

The only way to avoid taking up all the tiles in the large kitchen/diner/sitting room was to re-route the pipes around the outside of the house! This cost six hundred euros, which we felt was 'not quite cricket', since Maurice and Roy must have known about the leak.

In his younger days, Roy had worked for a couturier in London. He spoke at any opportunity about 'dressing Yana', a singer who had become a household name in the late 1950s. And it was obviously Roy who had designed the décor for the house. He had chosen a Spanish style, with tiled floors and wrought-iron arched doorways, which in a cold house without heating was not the best way to conserve heat.

The ground floor structure of a Normandy longhouse is basically two large rooms: historically, one to the right was used as the living quarters, the other to the left was for the cattle. We began to re-think everything, beginning with the ground floor. We found a wooden door manufacturer in nearby Gavray and chose a glass panel version to replace the wrought-iron between rooms.

We liked the tiling in the main room, but in the second room, we overlaid the tiles with carpet, which made it much cosier. The construction of this second room was strange. There was a 'mezzanine' at the near end, which Maurice had used as an office, and a space right up to the roof at the other. We had decided on first viewing that we would reconfigure the room to make a third en-suite bedroom upstairs.

We had arrived in October, so a main concern was heating. Our introduction to Robine was fortuitous as they were pioneers in ground source heating – geothermy – which was an obvious direction for us to go. We had sufficient land for the necessary underground pipes. Otherwise it meant a large butane gas tank.

Robine offered to install the system by Christmas if we could decide to go ahead the following day, but we felt we could not commit so quickly. Although the French government would refund a quarter of the outlay - as an incentive to install an environmentally-friendly system - the costs were still huge: twenty thousand euros, which included seventeen radiators. When we finally went ahead, we had to wait until February.

In the meantime, Maurice came over to give us a twenty minute lecture on how to light the wood burner! We grew to like Maurice a lot. He had such a fascination for facts, we did wonder sometimes if he was a little on the autistic spectrum. He knew the leaving point and destination of every plane that flew over Le Perrey. He also read UK train timetables for fun.

Maurice was helpful in administrative matters; how to go about things in this hugely bureaucratic society. The centre for administration was the Prefecture in St Lo, where we registered the details of our residency for local tax purposes as well as our car details. We did eventually exchange our driving licences for French ones.

It was also Maurice who gave us the history of our house in WW2. We discovered that Normandy drew a lot of World War Two enthusiasts, and the locals still had memories, or those passed down orally. Villedieu, thanks to the foresight of the mayor who contacted the American commander of the invasion force, was saved from allied bombing, unlike huge swathes of Normandy.

Apparently, early on our house and outbuildings had been searched by the Germans who were manning a lookout post on our hillside. They suspected it was a hiding place for resisters, but it proved empty, so they marked a swastika on our shed door, which was still vaguely visible.

The allied invasion had come from the St Sever direction, across the bocage towards us. At the time Le Perrey was 'the big house' and some of the locals were sheltering inside. The troops were making for a German trench nearby but in fact an advancing tank blew the end of our house off. That side was rebuilt and covered with stucco, unlike the rest of the building, which was original stone, and according to the date chiselled into the lintel of our stone fireplace was built in 1735.

Roy was a different matter. We came to understand that as far as he was concerned, we had taken over *his* house, and he somehow still had a right to hold sway. He was furious when a few months later we planned to demolish his kitchen and install one of our own. He sent Maurice to ask us for his old kitchen, which he used in their utility room.

Roy and Maurice invited us to tea several times, but Roy never quite forgave us. He refused to enter his old home, and on the one occasion I did persuade him to venture over, he sat outside with his back to the house.

Just before Christmas, on 16th December, I decided to take a day trip to Jersey. (It was also the day the three-phase electricity was installed in readiness for the geothermy.) The ferry left from the port of Granville, a twenty-eight kilometre drive away. Half-way across the engine broke down, and we were left 'bobbing about' helplessly for at least thirty minutes before it was fixed.

In fact, the trip was to meet my cousin Roz, who lived in St Helier. She was a tax exile there, but also had other homes in Spain and England. She had forged her way successfully to becoming a property developer, and although we had not seen much of each other over the years, this was the perfect opportunity.

I had not been to Jersey before, so Roz drove around to show me the sights, and then to her house for tea, before taking me back to the ferry. I noticed the people returning to Granville were laden with bags, and I was told later that this was how the Brits did their Christmas shopping. There was a big M & S in St Helier.

When the geothermy did arrive, it was amazing to watch. In the field bordering Christoff's land an enormous JCB carved out fifty yards of trench for the many pipelines, which held water with a drop of antifreeze. These led to a manifold at the top, and finally the one resulting pipe was drawn across a rockery into a large heat pump in the utility space at the side of our house.

It took another week or two to install the seventeen radiators. We knew we would never make our money back on this 'money-saving' system, but we loved the fact of this kind of heating, and it served us well. We were warned that when first switched on the heat was slow to take effect, but within twenty minutes the whole house felt deliciously warm.

Almost immediately I began a monthly commute to London. The slow local train from Villedieu took three hours to Paris Montparnasse, where I would take the metro to Gare du Nord. The Eurostar to London Waterloo arrived two hours later.

If I left at 6am I could be at work by the early afternoon, and when, a few years later, it was changed to St Pancras I was just five minutes' walk from Mary's flat. I stayed with Mary on occasion, but because her flat was small – and inconvenient to her for me to be there - it was more likely to be with Eileen.

I decided to research a new kitchen in Wembley Ikea. The Le Perrey kitchen was big: it needed cupboards along one wall and a centre workstation. On two or three visits I spent nine hours in total in the store, working out in fine detail the exact measurements for all the things we needed. Once I had done the spade work, we drove to the Nantes Ikea – a hundred and thirty-two miles from Beslon - to buy it all.

We worked hard to strip the old kitchen and wall tiles, but we also found Steve Bainton Smith to help us install it all. Steve was a flamboyant character who had appeared on the London stage, and also been a soldier and a musician in a military band.

He and his wife Cat, like many Brits we met, had decided to relocate to France to give their son Rufus a better education and lifestyle. To do this he had become what he called 'a Finisher'. A few years later he trained to be a chimney sweep which would be more lucrative for him. Cat worked in a French bank, providing necessary assistance to the many English-speaking residents. Rufus, at eight, was quite a character!

I like ex-pat living. It creates a culture where unlikely friendships can happen. We contacted Geoff and Pauline, who we had met on those earlier visits. Geoff had been a policeman in Newcastle and Pauline had run a pub. They had been together for many years, but never married.

They were renovating their house in Cherence-le-Heron near Ruffiny on the other side of Villedieu but were having a lot of bad luck with the French builders. They lost quite a lot of money in the process, but over the years the house gradually took shape.

Geoff and Pauline introduced us to friends Peter and Janet who lived in Villedieu. Peter had been a fire chief in Cambridgeshire and Janet, a police superintendent's daughter, had been a store detective, amongst other things. When we got to know them better, she confessed that one year she had had to arrest Father Christmas! Sue and Rob arrived in the area a little later and with their friends Janice and Alan we became 'the gang of ten'!

When I lived in Provence, I did have one or two French friends, but this was clearly not to be the case for us here. William was less practised in French than I was, and in any case, it felt to me that Normandy was like living in 'no-man's land' between France and England, and somehow it didn't matter. I was told that when the Brits moved in, the locals retired further south, some as far as Morocco.

As it happened, we met more local – Beslon – people at the annual village lunch. Held in July in a huge marquee set up in a field, the invitation came from the deputy mayor M. Bastard, who had a farm along our lane. It was an invitation we did not dare to refuse! For the villagers it was clearly the event of the year.

We took our own plates, knives and forks and lined up for the feast to be served. When the long tables began to fill up, we were guided to 'the English table' with the other ex-pats - except for Maurice and Roy who would not be marshalled and sat alone elsewhere.

That first year it was good to talk. We met a young couple: Scott, a builder, and his wife Debi, who became good friends. They lived further down the road towards Beslon with their two young children Sydney and Jessica. We also met Peter and Irina, ten or so years younger than us. Irina was Russian and for the most part lived in Moscow, teaching English, but mainly to look after her ageing parents.

She and Peter, who had a science background, had been together for many years, including some time teaching in Togo, but were not yet married. The distance relationship apparently suited them, because Irina, who spoke good English, was not keen on France, and Peter did not want to live in Russia. Irina, who did beautiful patchwork quilts for their house, would come to France at Easter, Christmas, and in the summer.

We became friends in a strange but lasting way. 'Silent Peter', who had originally come to France with his sister Lyn, would often sit without saying a word, responding with 'Um' rather than entering into the to and fro of the conversation. He was more comfortable with William, who could stand the silence, while I would end up chattering away, compelled to fill the gaps, until I felt I was speaking gibberish! But we managed.

Peter had two cats Billy and Squeaky, which William would occasionally go down to feed if Peter was away. But it was not long before we had Milly, a partly feral grey cat, rescued from abandonment and given by friends to Scott and Debi. Knowing we wanted a cat, Debi suggested we take her 'on appro'.

Milly had already had kittens, so we knew she had to neutered. She was never a lap cat, but she was our cat now, and we dealt with the regular rescue of mice she brought in to play with. We put her food, her bed, and the cat flap - in the garden room next to the kitchen.

We began to find our way around, eventually able to cross country and know where we were going. Our favourite 7am breakfast treat was The Dinandier, near the St Pierre Hotel in Villedieu, owned by Marie-Claude and her son Mikhail. They served the best *café au lait* for me and '*Le Yorkshire*' for William. We brought in croissants from Mme Javelet, the best (in our view) of the four patisseries and bought yesterday's '*Daily Telegraph*' (or '*Daily Mail*') from the Maison de Presse. Our perfect morning.

Villedieu-les-Poêles was predominantly a one-street town with parking down the middle; in some ways like Marlborough, except the natural stone was a darker colour. But turning left at the *rondpoint* you came to a large car park, which on Tuesdays took the overspill of the marvellous market. Here was the bank, the post office and, for those who preferred a more modern venue, The Fruitier Hotel.

The best 'find' of all was the French health system - and Dr Sesboue, our amazing local GP. It was the most personal relationship with a doctor we had ever had; attested by everyone we knew. He was quite simply 'a good man'. When the husband of a friend was dying, he visited the hospital every day, sitting at the back of the room while his wife was at his bedside. He listened, he acted, he furthered, and he cared; all with a fantastic dry sense of humour. He was Catholic, and every year took a party to Lourdes.

We had five acres of grassland and realised early on that this took quite a lot of management. Much to Roy's distain we did not keep horses, but instead bought a ride-on mower, from a showroom near St Lo, and William was in his element. It took eight hours to mow all the grass!

We had warned Maurice and Roy that we would have to take out the nineteen leylandii they had planted along our side of the boundary, because we could not stand them. When we did this, not to be daunted, they planted a series of trees on their own side. Fortunately, not Leylandii.

At the end of Spring, we asked a local English builder to design and build the third en-suite bedroom over the cathedral-like space in the second room. Before it was finished William's nephew Paul and his girlfriend (now his wife) Charrity, called in on their way back from a holiday in France. They were happy to put sleeping bags down in the unfinished room for the children: Charlie, Grace and Charrity's seven year old daughter Faye, while William taped up the windows to prevent them falling out!

We spent much of our time re-decorating, and I asked Hannah if I could pay her to make our curtains, which she was happy to do. But we did have time for one of the many local summer fairs held not far from us in La Colombe. We met Debi and Scott and enjoyed seeing Sydney, aged four, taking a donkey ride, and watching the enormous buffalos pulling carts.

We visited our first Normandy beach, Omaha, and wandered around the deeply moving American cemetery in Coleville sur Mer, where Theodore Roosevelt, the oldest man in the invasion, is remembered. He died of a heart attack on 12th June, just six days after the landing,

We now had space for visitors and were happy to drive the sixty miles to Caen ferry port to pick people up. Jan and Barrie came in September 2008 for Jan's sixtieth birthday. A favourite excursion for her was pottering around the Saturday market in Granville, where she bought a skirt, and some red and white sneakers, which she says still wears today! As a former fashion journalist, she also had to visit the Dior house museum on the cliff above the beach.

This was one of our favourite places. We would park near the museum and descend the vast number of steps to the promenade beside the beach. We would walk towards the town and back, proud we could manage the steps!

My friend Naiad from way back, also came to see us. She was now living in Pembrokeshire in a cottage on the land bought by her mother as a family enterprise. An avid gardener, she offered to prune the beautiful old, perfumed rose on the side of the large shed beyond our house, which in earlier times had been used as a chicken house. She also left us an unexpected legacy: an introduction to her old friends Simon and Ingrid de Lautour.

CHAPTER TEN

Autumn 2008-December 2010: Le Perrey 2

"Friends and visitors"

On her return home Naiad remembered that Simon and Ingrid De Lautour lived in St Vigor des Monts, a village not far from us. She had been at school with Simon's sister, actress Frances de la Tour, and they had then 'hung out' as a group in Windsor in their teenage years. Ingrid had been the Swedish au pair in his parents' home before she married Simon. Naiad gave us their number.

When I spoke to Simon on the phone, he told me that he and Ingrid had lived in Normandy for eight years, and before that in Provence for twenty years – in a village called Le Castellet! The synchronicity was extraordinary. We had both lived in Le Castellet at the same time and had never met!

As a former racing driver Simon had run a training school for drivers at the Le Castellet circuit, and his son now owned a restaurant in Sanary, a nearby seaside town. From now on we became friends in a loose kind way, with invitations to our homes for lunch, or, more often, meeting for lunch in a favourite local restaurant Les Bruyeres.

In November that year, 2008, having said I would never fly again, we did take a four-day holiday flight to the Algarve in Portugal. It was new to us both and a little strange to visit Praia da Luz, only a year after the disappearance of Madeleine

McCann. We had left from my aunt Eileen's house in East Barnet and returned there to collect our car before driving to a B & B for William's nephew Richard's wedding to Julianne in Haywards Heath.

That had been the plan! The evening before we left Portugal, we had eaten a curry, which within forty eight hours had 'done for me'. I was too ill to go to the wedding but for William, only mildly affected, it was a wonderful family gathering. (Incidentally, I have not flown since).

We took the opportunity to take Eileen back to France for a week-long visit. She loved the land and the horses and became fond of Gertie, Maurice and Roy's goat. By agreement, Gertie had stayed on our land so she could continue to use the tumble-down stone building beyond the gite as her shelter.

I took Eileen back by train to coincide with my monthly work date, but at the age of eighty-eight the walk between Montparnasse Gare and the metro proved too onerous. We didn't do that again.

That year we began our regular Christmas Eve 'party'. We invited Maurice, as we knew Roy would not come, Geoff and Pauline, Janet and Peter, Scott and Debi, and Peter and Irina, to 'drinks and nibbles'. It was fun.

On Christmas morning we joined three or four of the 'gang' for their annual Christmas Day meeting for mulled wine (or hot chocolate) at the Dinandier. We then returned home for our own ritual Christmas lunch: Confit de Canard, the famous Cedilla on Provençal favourite, which comes in a tin!

In Winter it invariably snowed to a greater or lesser extent, and M. Bastard would plough the lane in a marvellous neighbourly gesture. But one morning, a London work-day, it was four feet high in our drive, so William and I carried my bag on a pole between us and ploughed our way through. We then trudged along the tractor tyre tracks to the tarmac road, which was clear, and Peter Thompson kindly drove me to the station.

It was lovely to watch the horses in Maurice and Roy's fields in the snow, but they were also proud to show us the lambs that were born towards the Spring. Little did we imagine that soon we would have two sheep of our own.

During that year, William cleared the walled vegetable garden in front of the gite, which Maurice and Roy had let go, and set up a system of raised beds. It was the first opportunity since Fourways to indulge his love of growing. I planted and maintained the borders around the house.

In early Spring, Debi's friends Sabina and Simon who lived in Montbray, offered to give us two sheep from their flourishing flock. Sabina, an IT expert, had designed the labels for the CDs I now made for client sessions, as well as the headline banner for my flyers. We stood at the edge of their field and picked out 'our' two sheep, and Simon kindly brought them over in his van.

Tandy and Mags (our names) had the run of a large field, but with easy access to the back entrance of the former chicken shed. And then we discovered they were pregnant! We kept in touch with Sabina and Simon, and one day in early March, when they drove over to see us with their two young boys Connor and Archie, a lamb was born before our eyes!

To our amazing good fortune, the three lambs (two for Mags, one for Tandy) were born without assistance. (Cybele came over for the afterbirths!). Ba, Cider and Pom were one of the nicest things to happen to us in Le Perrey. They were fed by their mothers and lived in and out of the shed. They would follow us in for feed when necessary.

The lambs were at their most delightful when a group came in late March for my first four-day workshop in Le Perrey: *'Knowing our place in a changing world'*. On this occasion the participants all travelled by train and we could pick them up in Villedieu. We had a twin room and a double room for guests Jo and Barbara, and Debi and Scott had a two bedroom gite for three sharing.

Three participants, Cecile, a French woman living in Scotland, Mary Robinson, now a regular, and Jan – who was a long-term client, registered blind - shared an apartment in Courson nearby. (We named them the Renegades when they borrowed William's car one evening and went out for a jolly to a local bar!)

I had planned menus for lunches and cooked in advance, but it was hugely helpful that Debi came for an hour each day to set it up, and she and William washed up afterwards.

It became established practise for two participants each day to buy and cook food for the evening meal. William would drive them down to the Casino supermarket in the later afternoon, though trying to get them back on time, he said, was 'like herding school children'!

In the workshops, we experienced how in a 'new order' it is not hierarchy or social positioning that matter. It is simply the pleasure of people evolving individually, generationally and collectively to their highest potential.

We had a great time, including an outing to Mont St Michel, where we walked along the causeway contemplating the work we had been doing. We also went to a beach near Granville. Cecile made the meal on the last evening, which was a *tour de force* and a fitting conclusion to the workshop.

Once again Jan and Barrie had offered their house during their annual holiday in Greece, and in June - because several people had expressed interest in the themes of the workshop in France - I went to London to hold a similar weekend: "*Who am I, Who are You? Knowing our place in a changing world.*"

The following weekend I held another two days: *'Meaning in the 21st Century',* which looked at where we were heading, individually and collectively, at this time of major change and disruption.

Back home in France, the vegetables were growing, the flowers were flourishing, and several people came to visit that summer. Duncan, a friend from Ramsbury whose wife had sadly died, stayed with us for a few days. Also, Mel and Steve, and Hannah.

Some of our visitors, like Elisabeth and James preferred to stay in a nearby hotel. Le Manoir, in the countryside outside Villedieu was favourite, with its Michelin star chef. This was also the choice of John and Barbara, and, a little later, of William's sister Kathleen (Tass) and husband David.

Elisabeth and James had driven up by car from Roussillon, and were with us when James, the son of William's cousin Ros, called by for lunch with his family. Later, Elisabeth and I took a boat trip to explore the Isles de Chaussey, fifteen miles from Granville, while the men stayed at home to watch Formula 1, and James cooked William a fry-up

By now we had established our preference for lunches and teas rather than going out for an evening meal. We met Pauline and Geoff, Janet and Peter, and Sue and Rob on various occasions in each other's houses. We saw a lot of Scott and Debi, and particularly enjoyed the frequent English language films at the Rex cinema in Villedieu, where Peter was volunteer projectionist.

I went regularly to the swimming pool in Villedieu, but most important, I had found a hairdresser I liked. I saw a woman with my kind of hair at a Christmas Fair and asked her where she went. She recommended Isabelle, who owned a salon in Agon-

Coutainville, a seaside town near Coutances. It was worth the thirty mile drive each way.

In the autumn of 2009, I came back from an appointment with Isabelle, to find William lying on his bed. That morning he had met Steve Bainton Smith in Gavray to sort out an order for a patio door, when he felt anxious and uncomfortable, 'a bit not there'. Steve, obviously worried, had said 'you look ill. Are you going to die on me?'

William drove home, made a cup of tea, managed the stairs and tried to relax, hoping to feel better after a sleep. When I got home, it was clear he had had another stroke, and I went into action. I called the emergency sappeurs pompiers, who carry out fire and ambulance duties in France, and they sent a four-man crew. When they saw the stairs, they called a second crew and, strapped onto a stretcher, eight burley men manoeuvred William down the staircase.

I followed the vehicle and met him in casualty where he was put on a trolley in the emergency room. Soon after, he was given an ex-ray and two hours later was taken to the surgical ward, and I went home.

This stroke impaired William more than before. The following morning, he had paralysis in his right foot, his leg was stiff and his hand too. His speech was affected, and he found it more difficult to say some words. But by the end of the week, transferred to the medical ward, he was able to limp around.

The doctors – so much more accessible than in the UK – sat down with us at the end of the corridor and showed us the ex-ray where we could see the tiny hole in William's brain. The answer to all our questions about the prognosis was 'take time, go steady and allow improvements to take shape in their own time'.

And that is how it was. He worked hard on his leg, and every day he wrote out the alphabet many times to exercise his hand. The hardest task was his diction, when words would not come out right. For a while Maurice, in particular, found this difficult, and he would turn and talk to me.

Although it took more effort than last time, the improvements came steadily and surely. I encouraged William to plant some beans, even though, when he eventually got down on his knees, he stumbled on the way up and fell backwards into the raspberry canes. But we laughed.

He started walking every day, the same routine along the lane, telephone pole to telephone pole. If he dawdled or chatted to a neighbour, I would get worried and appear at the gate, or text the mobile, which he always promised to carry. After a while, Cybele would crawl under the gate and walk alongside him. This seemed to annoy Roy, but it made no difference; Cybele got out somehow.

Although William still felt 'out of place' and his balance had deteriorated, things did go back to a 'new normal'. His speech improved and, as he says in his book: '*So You've Had a Stroke*', published in 2017, he only went back to 'stroke speech' if he was stressed or nervous.

On the plus side, he says, it seemed to have changed his personality. His quick fire temper had gone, and to his amazement he no longer found life so challenging. He now had a much calmer worldview. And despite his slight impairment we could still enjoy our favourite walks: in the St Sever forest, or the four kilometers around the Dathee lake, near Vire.

Early in 2010 I had the idea to visit Fish Hoek. Although I had been to South Africa many years earlier, I had never been Cape Town. A friend from Le Castellet days, Soozi Holbeche, had returned to Fish Hoek with her South African husband

Dennis and we had stayed in touch. It was agreed I would stay in a B & B, do some exploring, but would also do some private sessions in her home. It was all settled. I made a flyer which she would disperse, and, yet again breaking my vow, booked the flight for mid-April.

The weekend before I was due to go, I attended a course on hand-frame weaving at West Dean College of Arts and Conservation near Chichester. I had begun weaving at an evening class when we lived in Kew and loved it. During the course at West Dean, we made a small runner under instruction, which I still have.

But then, towards the end of the weekend, the news came through that there was a volcanic eruption in Iceland, which was causing enormous disruption to air travel. Checking it on the College internet, I knew that was the end of my trip to Cape Town. No more flying needed.

In May, my cousin Chris came to Le Perrey to celebrate her sixtieth birthday. She and husband John slept in their camper van, while son Roger pitched a tent (to Cybele's great excitement) and daughter Emma and husband Andy made first use of the gite.

In June I held a five-day workshop *'Remember Me, Who I Am: moving the planet forward.'* We were a smaller group: Elisabeth, Brenda, Barbara and Jo, which was lovely for me. We could cover a lot of ground, individually and together, take excursions, and have quiet times. Elisabeth made it her daily mission to collect the sheep dung in the wheelbarrow and deliver it to the compost heap in the veg garden!

One evening during the workshop, a vast swarm of bees arrived and entered the cracks and crevices in the stonework, as well the eaves of the house. They seemed quite benign, but I rang the local bee man, who reassured us they were too busy to do us any harm.

Apparently, when bees are ready to swarm, they try a few possible sites beforehand. If they came back the next day, he said, he would come and take the swarm away, but as they didn't return, we assume we not a suitable venue!

Later that month I had my own difficulties. I went dizzy! So much so, that I stayed in bed for three weeks. I remember the timing well because I listened to the radio all day, following moment by moment the 2010 election. It was the year conservative David Cameron was elected but without sufficient seats. This led to intense negotiations for a coalition, eventually with the Liberal Democrats under the leadership of Nick Clegg.

Having to look after me, William's cooking skills improved no end, and he exercised his legs constantly going up and down stairs. At the end of three weeks we called the surgery. Dr Sesboue came and checked me over, but there was nothing obvious to see. Gradually I got back to normal life, although for several months my head could feel 'strange'. By coincidence, Elisabeth also went dizzy, and for her too, the condition lingered for a long time.

Later that Autumn, while staying with Eileen in London for work, the dizziness overtook me again. The local pharmacy suggested I call 111, which directed me to a local hospital. The consultant finally diagnosed Labyrinthitis and gave me suitable pills, which was really helpful. Eventually over the months – and maybe years - the 'head' business did finally settle. Since then I have only had one other three-week bout in bed, and on that occasion seasickness pills helped.

The highlight of July was sheep-shearing. Two men did the rounds of all the local farms. We paid them ten euros per sheep, and they took the fleece away. Later that year we asked Sabina and Simon to take Ba, Cider and Pom back to their smallholding. With one male and two female lambs we knew we could not manage. A short time after that, to our surprise, they called in with a joint for the freezer. We didn't dare ask who it was!

That year William had a project. In the mid-eighties Libby Cross had been a presenter on '*Same Difference*', his series on disability for Channel 4. Libby was a wheelchair user following an accident on a motorbike at the age of seventeen. She had gone on to become a radio producer for programmes such as '*Archive on Four*', but they had stayed in touch. (We had been invited to her wedding to Matt in 2008: a lovely occasion on HMS Warrior in Portsmouth harbour.)

As a high profile disabled woman, Libby had now been asked by the Spinal Injuries Association to make three promotional films. She contacted William to be cameraman and editor, and after his stroke he was pleased to go back to work. He stayed with Eileen in East Barnet for an extended period and travelled to meet Libby on location.

He edited some of the material in France, and then returned with the equipment to East Barnet to complete, but it was a tough assignment and William became more and more anxious. Making the DVD for the final programme proved to be the last straw.

One morning he was driving to Cirencester to see a production company for advice, when he suddenly felt ill and had to pull up on the grass verge of a roundabout. Eventually he was sick out of the car door. Thirty minutes later a kindly German woman stopped her car to ask if he was all right. All he managed to say was 'No. Hospital', and she called an ambulance. He had had his third stroke.

A policeman asked William if he could contact anyone, and this man phoned me in France. He also drove the car to Emma's address, and William was on a stretcher in Great Western Hospital's A and E when Emma came to sit with him. As before, his blood pressure had gone sky high, but at that moment, he says, the weight of the video and the DVD lifted off. He knew he could not do it and felt a million times better.

At home in France, anxious once again, I ramped up. I booked an overnight ferry and Maurice knew exactly which trains in Portsmouth would tally with my arrival. I phoned Kenny, the owner of the Kingsbury B & B in Swindon to book a room. We often stayed at Kenny's which, as luck had it, was next door to the hospital.

I took the train to Caen and a taxi to Ouistreham ferry port. Sleeping overnight in a normal recliner seat was impossible with all the snoring around me, but the trains worked well, and I went straight to the hospital. Five days later we collected the car and returned home, armed yet again with a dizzying array of pills. Thankfully, the impairments were only slightly more than before.

CHAPTER ELEVEN

January 2011-October 2013: Le Perrey 3

'Time to Change'

By the beginning of 2011, I had begun writing a channelled book: *'Time to Change: a guide to life after greed'*. My opening to spiritual awareness, and what I might then have called Jung's 'Superconscious', had begun in the mid-seventies. I 'knew' this journey for me was about two things. Firstly, understanding and experiencing the emergence of 'the feminine principle'. I believed the over-riding task of humanity was the integration of spirit and matter, in order to unravel a little more of the great mystery of what it is to be human.

I also 'knew' it was about Greed and that the purpose of this era was to establish the resonance of loving kindness and equality. The meaning for me – and what I felt I could offer my clients - was the experience of the evolution of consciousness.

In 1977 I had written about the 'spiritual feminine' in *'The Wise Virgin'* (published in 1979), and finally I was doing the greed book. For the next few months, I would wake at 4am every morning and sit in my bed to channel directly onto the computer: a short chapter a day.

Like many in my field I trusted the idea that 2012 was a special year. According to different beliefs – including New Age (as Mind, Body, Spirit was called in the early days) - it would begin a period of positive transformation, a new era, marked by astrological alignments. I liked the idea that my book should coincide with this. I approached my literary agent from years ago and she suggested O Books, who published the book in December 2011.

But publishing is so different now. Long gone are the days when a publisher accepted the book and all you had to do was read the galley proofs. Today, even with a publisher, unless you are a truly established author, you are expected to choose the cover, do the cover text, and then embark on the marketing yourself; on social media and by reaching large audiences through tours or talks. All conversation with O Books was on the publisher's 'Forum', and nothing personal. We decided in the future to publish ourselves.

2011 was a busy year. In January, Sophia and Jeremy came to stay to celebrate Jeremy's sixtieth birthday. In April we went to London for Eileen's ninetieth. I ordered a cake and invited several of her friends to an afternoon tea party. Her son, my cousin Alan, came over from the Philippines with Jill, a Philippina work colleague who was setting up a London office for him.

And in May - as tech-averse as I was - I decided to create a website. I had seen a site I liked, found the designer, and on another trip to the UK we went to see Zoe who lived near Ashford in Kent. We commissioned a WordPress design, as a means to advertise the book and also as a platform to offer the work.

In June I held a one-day workshop at Jan and Barrie's in London, based on *'Time to Change',* and in July, on another visit to the UK, Mel and Steve invited us to their home for a pre-publication celebration with home-made cupcakes. In August, Peter and Irina were married and held a wedding celebration lunch at their home. Paul, Charrity and family called by again.

The website went live in August 2011, with William in charge of the technical side (an amazingly fast learning curve for him). I began a monthly channelling which – apart from a short sabbatical in 2012 - I have done ever since and established an archive. More recently I have added an audio meditation, and now a Podcast.

At the beginning of September, Jenny Sharp, the closest friend and power of attorney to Peggy Smallbone in Bovey Tracey, asked me to come over, at Peggy's request. She was now very ill and confined to bed with full-time care. I had visited Peggy regularly since my friend Vlyn's death, but this was a strange moment. I stayed a few days and then returned home. Peggy died a week or so later, and I went back again for her funeral.

Also, in September, William's niece Sarah and husband J-P came down and stayed in the Fruitier hotel in Villedieu. It was after their bi-annual American Boy Scout camp in Normandy and before they went on to visit J-P's French family.

But we were thinking again of our future. We loved Le Perrey and despite Roy's dire predictions, we felt we had managed the land well, but we did have to admit defeat with Tandy and Mags.

An important part of sheep care was to regularly cut their hooves, and this meant hauling the sheep onto their backs, which neither of us could manage. We began to rely on Maurice more and more, and eventually felt this was unfair. We were both sad when we decided to ask Sabina and Simon to take them back.

The vegetable garden was also becoming a problem. Through the strokes William's balance had been compromised. He could no longer get down on the ground; or rather, it was difficult to get up once he was down there. I was in charge of harvesting the produce, but now I also had to do more of the planting.

We decided that rather than down-size in France, we should do the 'sensible' thing and return to the UK. For William, more than for me, this was fine. He missed the general 'chit chat' he could have in English – like in supermarket queues - which was not possible for him in French. We set in motion the sale of Le Perrey, though we knew it could take a very long time. In fact, it took over two years.

At the end of that year my sister-in-law died, aged sixty-nine of lung cancer, which changed things in the most amazing way. After eleven years of estrangement from my brother and his family, we were totally surprised to be invited to Margaret's funeral and natural burial near their home in East Sussex.

Our welcome was extraordinary. Mike and his children, Matthew and Karen particularly, but also Clare, went out of their way to include us and sit with us at the wake. This is when it became apparent that it was Margaret who had instigated the difficulties between us, and very soon afterwards Mike came to stay in France.

That first year we visited sites according to his wishes, like Mont St Michel and Granville, or those geared to his passion for geocaching. We trailed after him while he searched for his 'treasure', and William in particular enjoyed being initiated into the mysteries of this pursuit.

We learned early on just to follow Mike's lead – he had always made a plan – and from then on, he would visit us every three or so months. Even when, the following year, he married Di, twelve years younger, in July 2013. He would come on his own while she was house-sitting for her clients.

Four years older than me, Mike now seemed to enjoy our company. He and I had never talked much, and he was quite a silent man, but over the following years I pushed for some 'straight talking'. We spoke our truth about our childhoods and how different our pictures were, and surprised as we were by that, we became much closer.

His own path had been a highly successful career with Lloyds of London, and he had three high-achieving children. My life was so different and he more or less dismissed – or ignored - it, until, grudgingly, he opened to the fact, if not the letter, of what I did. I think, in the end, he did feel just a little proud – maybe! A visit from Mike always ended with an invitation to a curry at the best place available, and we looked forward to it.

In November I held another one-day workshop based on the book, this time in the Wellbeing Clinic in Marlborough, run by Jill, a friend of David Furlong. She was happy to advertise the event which brought new people.

Over the years in Le Perrey I had begun to do some short trips on my own, visiting various places that caught my interest: like St Malo and Dinan - where I took a river trip - and William the Conqueror's 12th Century castle: Chateau de Falaise. I also met Hannah, and later Janice, in Paris, and visited an art gallery near Gare du Nord, now owned by cousin Chris's nephew Joe, who had emigrated from Australia.

And on my way back from working in London, I also took train trips from Paris. On one nostalgic visit to Geneva, I arranged to meet Susan Souter, a regular workshop participant and now a friend. She lived with her husband Ian in Lausanne, and we arranged to meet in La Rippe, north of Nyon. This is where I had lived with my partner Austin in the mid-eighties, when I worked at WHO.

On another occasion I took the train to Munich and explored the town. I was shocked enough to see the door of Hitler's office, but the day after a train trip to Dachau concentration camp, I felt really sick and unwell. The best place by far was Monet's Garden in Giverny, which is easily reached by train from Paris, and I have been there twice.

'Time to Change' came out in December, and in January 2012 I held another workshop at Jan's in Southfields: 'Launching into 2012'. We looked, again, individually and collectively, at 'the promised moment of change'.

In May, William's oldest granddaughter Lauren was eighteen, and we now established the idea of eighteenth birthday excursions. For Lauren, an alumnus of the Sylvia Young Stage School, we suggested lunch and a performance of: 'Of Mice and Men' at the Watermill Theatre, Newbury. She was keen to see it: a play she had studied for A levels, but the thing she remembers most about the lunch is that we plied her with questions – a journalistic habit!

We continued to enjoy meeting up with the neighbours. June 2012 was the Queen's Diamond Jubilee. We celebrated with lunch at our house, and the guests (Peter, Janet and Pauline) came bearing large union jacks! And in July was the 'Great Rite of the Knights of Malta', a ceremony that took place in Villedieu every four years.

Villedieu-les-Poeles had been founded in 1130 by the Hospitaliers of the Order of St John of Jerusalem, and evidence of the Commanderie is still there. Later named the Order of Malta, the original mission of the wounded knights returning from Jerusalem after crusades, was to 'welcome, nurse and save the weakest'. The Great Rite was an extraordinary event. Everyone in the town and around turned out; the streets were garlanded with white flags with the black Maltese cross.

The Knights of Malta, heavily clad in black robes with the cross embroidered on the front, processed around the town with their icon of Mary. Ordinary clergy, children in white robes, interested citizens and the general public followed as we watched. Today the Knights of Malta do good works, but as we looked at the faces of these men - and thought of the secrecy of such orders - they did look a bit sinister.

In the summer of 2012, we valiantly attended the village lunch, but by then we were on our own – the other Brits, including Maurice and Roy, had given up. This time we were seated alone in the middle of M. Bastard's party, all speaking French around us. Since no one took any notice of us at all, we made a plan to talk to each other, with great animation, throughout the meal. We then decided to abandon ship like the rest of the British contingent.

In late Autumn we did something neither of us had done before. We went to the UK and took a trip to Blackpool to see the lights! We stayed in Lytham St Anne's, ate fish and chips with mushy peas, took the tram to the end of the line at Fleetwood. On our return to Blackpool, we sat in the 'champagne bar' which did not sell champagne, and looked out at the lights. We loved it.

Just before Christmas 2012, William's daughters Emma and Mel made the surprising decision to do a day-return visit. They took the overnight ferry from Portsmouth to Caen, where we picked them up at 5am for a café breakfast. We then drove them home for lunch, and after a whirlwind day dropped them back for the 6pm return. They stayed overnight in Portsmouth.

In January 2013, looking for a space to hire in London at a reasonable rate, I booked a room at the College of Psychic Studies, for a one-day workshop: '*Waking Up to Ourselves: What did happen in 2012?*' It was seventeen years since my one year employment at the College, and the energy was still not quite right. But the workshop itself went well.

To our delight we were invited by Matthew and Samantha - Mike's son and wife - and their children, William and Emily, to their house-warming lunch party in Bodiam. Mary, who has always been a favourite with my family, was there too. Matthew's meteoric rise through the ranks, to CEO of a Lloyds broker has meant riches along the way.

I remember his wish as a child to be a landscape gardener and in a way he is. He can landscape his large estate, with B & Bs, and guest cottage, to his heart's content. His pride and joy is a motor museum; a large building with ten vintage cars, all of which he can and does take out to drive.

In June I held our last five-day workshop in Le Perrey: *'The Way We Live Now'*. I felt now that all the personal groundwork had been done – at least in the sense of my evolving workshops. At this point I wanted to "explore individually and collectively the reach of human possibilities within the framework of loving kindness".

Unusually Hannah came to this workshop. On the whole she preferred not to work in a group setting but thank goodness she did. William and I decided to stay in the gite and give the run of the main house over to the group. On this occasion they prepared their own evening meals, and William and I stayed separate. But each day it seemed this arrangement imprisoned William in a way that made him increasingly anxious.

On the last day of the workshop, I was holding our first session, when I saw William walking past the window, clearly in trouble, and needing to find me. He had been to town but had felt unwell. Immediately I called the sappeur pompiers, and while we waited, I called Hannah to give William some healing in the hope to calm him.

When the *Sami* – emergency - Dr arrived, there was a long process of deciding what to do. Eventually William was taken by ambulance to A & E at Avranches, and I was told I could come at 2pm.

Knowing there was nothing I could do until then, it felt easier to continue with the group and take my mind off things, but when I left at lunchtime to drive to the hospital, I asked Hannah to take over. She did it willingly and offered the group an experience of the Alexander Technique.

It felt surreal. I found William in a ward where he stayed for four days. This time he had had a TIA, but it seemed, once again, he was only there for supervision while they monitored his blood pressure. The following day, Barbara's husband Dave arrived to take Barbara and Mary back to the UK, while Peter Thompson kindly agreed to drive three others to Rennes airport. I could then turn back to concentrate on William.

William's one abiding memory is that each day the other man in his room donated his pudding to him! And that most of the time he was starving. I, on the other hand, was utterly exhausted, and on the one day I just couldn't move to visit, Peter and Janet kindly offered. William says they walked him up and down the corridor for exercise.

The reason for my exhaustion - apart from recovering from the workshop – was that while William was in hospital, I was cleaning the house from top to toe. I was also filling some cracks in the gite, because potential buyers, Mike and Chris, were coming to see our property for a second time.

Our attempt to sell Le Perrey had not gone well. One man from Germany came several times, but after a while we viewed him as a 'property tourist' and knew he would never buy. We changed from one estate agent to another and tried an on-line approach; still with no joy. Finally, we put the house into the hands of Sheila, a charming young freelance woman, attached to an agency in Brittany. She went into bat for us and eventually succeeded.

Mike and Chris had sold their house in Wales after six years and were looking for a large property in France. They felt we were not quite big enough for their needs - they had several horses and a trap - and were not in the right location, but they came once and were clearly tempted. Sheila told them they would have to pay full price because the market was buzzing which, having waited over two years to sell, we thought was brilliant negotiation! They bought the house.

A short time later they came again and had tea with Maurice and Roy. The land, according to Roy, was meant for horses, so this was his dream team - although it didn't take long for them to fall out of favour!

While they were there, I was anxious to deflect the noise of the A84 motorway, which you could hear when the wind was blowing in the wrong direction. I suggested to William that he mow the lawn, which he did for about two hours! It was never mentioned!

When William came home from hospital, he had a little less physical ability, though he could still mow the grass, which made him very happy. For the first time he used a stick to aid his balance, but as he was to discover when he joined a stroke club in the UK, he had been very lightly touched.

A visit by William's cousin Ros and her husband Colin was very welcome. Colin had had a series of heart attacks some years earlier and was now a little less able. William's brother John had recently established a 'cousins' lunch', which had renewed his connection to Ros and another cousin Eddie, and we enjoyed their company.

We had decided to return to Marlborough. Although we realised that there was limited availability in our price range, we found a bungalow on a small estate, ten minutes' walk from the town. After the space and horizons of Le Perrey this would be very different. William predicted it would only be for two years – an intuition which proved correct.

After Mike and Di's wedding in July 2013, we returned to complete our time at Le Perrey. Debi had already left France with the children, leaving Scott behind. She had finally come to the end of her tether and, as much as anything, wanted to return to her work as a beautician. We continued to see Scott, until he too went home, and they eventually got back together.

Sue and Rob left before us. They, too, were ready to 'go home'. They planned to live with their son and daughter-in-law, in separate wings of a large property – a former nursing home. It suited them all to have a large project for renovation, including a business. We have stayed in touch. Our sadness was leaving Peter and Janet and Pauline.

A last outing was to Lisieux in the neighbouring Department of Calvados. The town was an important centre of power in medieval times, and the main judge of Joan of Arc became bishop of Lisieux after her death. The Basilica is dedicated to Sainte-Therese de Lisieux, who was beatified in 1923 and cannonized in 1925.

A dilemma for us, before leaving France, was Milly, and the idea of taking her away from her vast roaming grounds to such a small environment. We had applied for her cat passport and were ready for travel, but suddenly there was another solution. Mike and Chris had just lost their much-loved cat and were happy to take her. (When we returned to visit a year or so later, she had obviously settled and completely ignored us!)

We left France in October 2013, and after an initial three weeks staying in a hotel in Weymouth, while waiting for vacant possession, we moved into 54 Priorsfield.

CHAPTER TWELVE

October 2013-October 2015: 54 Priorsfield

'The Interim'

On our first trip into town, we were chuffed to see the band of the Grenadier Guards marching up the High Street - which we chose to see as heralding our arrival!

Towards the end of our time in Le Perrey, my work life had changed considerably. Mary had retired and as a consequence had retired me. I no longer needed to commute from wherever we lived because, after seventeen years, I no longer had a London work-space. To hire a room at this stage was too uncertain, and to some extent I lost my London clientele.

However, I continued to go to London regularly. I would meet Mary and Jan and also Janice, my first client all those years ago at the College of Psychic Studies. Janice, a former BBC producer, had come to workshops in the early days, but not in recent years. We continued as friends, with occasional tune-ins when an issue came up.

But my main focus was Eileen, now in her mid-nineties. I would stay with her for a few days so I could keep an eye on how she was doing; collect her pension, do a little extra shopping, cook a few meals – and clean her oven! A neighbour Carla looked after her pride and joy, the garden, while Debbie would do her main shopping.

We also took Christmas to her in the following few years, until amazingly she was persuaded to travel to the Philippines at the age of ninety-six, to be admirably cared for by her beloved son Alan and his new young Philippina wife. Eileen died eighteen months later.

Alan described his mother as 'cool under fire'; nothing would rattle her. Several times when I asked if she was worried or stressed, she told me she did not understand what that was. I remember many years ago a friend of Vlyn's telling me she was not scared of flying because she 'didn't have that much imagination'.

Perhaps Eileen, a determined Aries, was the same, so I guess living the imaginative life is the downside for 'sensitives'! Imagination is all in the work I do. Guided meditation calls exclusively for the truth of the imagination, and that we trust what we perceive imaginatively: what we feel, see, or sense, is real.

With less client work I now concentrated on workshops. The loyal group of participants – now good friends – Elisabeth, Barbara, Susan, Brenda, Jo and several others were keen to move forward and continue working with the guides. They would still come from far and wide: France, Switzerland, London.

Elisabeth, who finally settled on Lizzie - which James always called her anyway - was always enthusiastic. Over the years she and I had worked – as did everyone – on the difficulties of her younger life and past life predispositions, but now she was emerging as a gifted channel.

We had established that until a certain moment she could not 'hear' wisdom (her own) through a woman. This means that however deeply a client sees into their dramas and experiences a sense of moving through them, the effect will not be permanent. There is an unconscious 'shan't' in the psyche – for past history reasons – when help comes through a woman, not a man! I have encountered this once or twice over the years.

When Lizzie saw this, things changed. Several years earlier she had withdrawn from Buddhism and the teachings of His Holiness. Her channelling went deeper into her being and the tone was hers not – in some strange way – Tibetan, as it had been.

The truth of her imagination was clear to us all, and for a long time I had felt that she, as a younger woman by seventeen years, would take the work further than I could. In later years we agreed to 'swap' channellings, and I trusted her guidance as much as my own.

At the same time, I did the monthly channelling for the website, which people could subscribe to. And in that sense, I was building a body of work. But one of our first priorities in Priorsfield was second granddaughter Immy's 18th birthday excursion. She chose lunch and a performance of *Nutcracker* at the Wyvern Theatre in Swindon. Immy was at college and training to be a beautician.

The good thing about Priorsfield was that we could easily walk to town and continue our early morning breakfast fix – by now we had switched to Costa! I joined the monthly U3A bird watching group - which I had done when we lived here before – with the same amazing expert Steve. To me this was the perfect way to explore the area and to have companionship for a walk.

Of course, William and I did walk together – often in the Savernake forest where we would take a picnic lunch - but as the strokes had taken effect his pace was markedly slower. As it happened, I was approached by Gill, a member of the bird watching group, who asked if I would like to join her for Sunday walks.

It was good to walk three, four, five miles at a stretch. She knew the area and would choose the venue, and then she led the way – though there were one or two occasions when we got lost and it was left to me had to retrace our steps! Gill was a former botany teacher, and for added interest she would point out plants along the way.

She lived alone and had suffered from depression – her NHS therapy was Mindfulness. Sadly, in the end, her constant negativity and judgemental attitude became too much for me. I felt I had to withdraw – on difficult terms. This meant leaving the bird-watching group as I felt she needed it more than I did.

Moving home so often means that friends are mostly 'elsewhere'! I have kept up friendships for many years, but they rarely live 'next door'. But one nice friend I made in Priorsfield was Linda, the neighbour opposite. With her partner John, we would get together for tea or chats, and they are friends to this day.

The trouble with writing a memoir is that you are obliged to age! In February 2014 it was William's 70th birthday. Being back in Marlborough, we lived near Emma, James and their family once again, and they could come to William's tea party. We also celebrated with a 'cousins' lunch', at Tass and David's local golf club in Hertfordshire, which could include their daughter Kathy. Ros produced a cake with candles.

The saddest thing for me, on 14th February that year, was the death of Myrna in France at the age of fifty-nine. Since we first met in Santorini in 1990, I had seen her almost every year, although 2010 and my fleeting visit before William's stroke, was the final time. Since then she had moved from Valensole to a favourite village Vaison-la-Romaine in the Vaucluse.

. Several years earlier, Myrna had suffered breast cancer, but it was a long time - and many complementary therapies later

- before she finally agreed to a mastectomy. When she fell ill again with terminal cancer, we spoke fairly often on the phone, but she would only talk of 'happy things' and I did not know how imminently serious it was.

It was a shock when Sophia rang to tell me that Myrna had died. We knew little of the circumstances and there was no mutual friend to tell us. I felt sad, but also upset, that our long friendship had ended so abruptly and not knowing the real context.

In March 2014 I hired a room at the Castle and Ball, a favourite pub/restaurant in Marlborough, for a one-day workshop: '*Why Would You Let Nature down?*', suggesting that the most important relationship we have at this time is to Nature, and the dire consequences of relinquishing that responsibility.

Lizzie, Susan, and Jo were there, as well as Christine, another long-time client who lived near Stroud. The plan was to experience themselves and each other, as the representatives of nature, and to see the natural world in a different light. At the end of the day, of course, we had tea and a lot of laughter.

That Spring William and I planned a trip to Liverpool. We travelled by National Express from London and stayed in a hotel near the centre. We walked round Albert Dock and went on 'the Beatles' tour'. We visited the Everyman theatre, the Catholic cathedral and had a meal in the Philharmonic Dining Rooms, the pub once favoured by John Lennon. We were intrigued to learn later that Barbara's husband Dave went to school with John Lennon!

We saw the Cavern Club – and were proud to see 'The Yardbirds' written on the back wall alongside the Beatles. James - of Lizzie and James - the drummer for this 70s band, still does hugely successful Yardbird tours as the only original member.

In fact, our 18th birthday excursion the following year with third grandchild Toby – a music enthusiast - was to be to a Yardbird gig in Frome, followed by a chat with the band and dinner afterwards with James. We also gave him a Yardbird LP.

Mike came for his regular visit and geocaching excursion. One outing was to Laycock Village - now owned almost exclusively by the National Trust. For our end of visit curry Mike took us to the Palm Restaurant, just outside Marlborough, a well-known 'go to' destination for Londoners.

In July 2014 we celebrated William's brother John's 80th birthday – at a lunch in a pub near their home in Warwickshire, and then a birthday cake tea at their home. This party now included William's other brother Mike and his wife Margaret, which brought them into our environment in a way they had not been before.

After a successful scientific career Mike and Margaret had left the family orbit and moved to Perth in Scotland to run a B & B. They had now relocated to be nearer their son Christopher in the Forest of Dean. We began to meet them 'half-way' for lunch - in Bath - where Mike had found a favourite art shop to buy materials for his new painting endeavours. Earlier, as an enthusiastic wildlife photographer, his work had been taken up by the Scottish tourist board.

Ros and Colin came to visit, and we also went to Villedieu for a few days. The ferry from Portsmouth to Caen was so convenient, and the drive the other side was only two hours. We stayed at the St Pierre. Normandy was still 'home' to me, and I think it always will be, and we have visited once or twice a year ever since.

We were invited to lunch by our buyers Mike and Chris, who had changed little inside the house but had made it somehow cosier. They had built a horse shelter for three horses (on top of the geothermy pipeline!) and made a *menege* – a horse training ring – in one of the fields. It was lovely to be back.

Since Rob and Sue were also visiting, we had lunch in our favourite restaurant Le Pussoir, with Janet and Peter, Janice and Alan and Pauline. Sadly, we were no longer the gang of ten, but the gang of nine. Just before we left Le Perrey, Geoff had had a heart attack and died, which was a terrible shock for us all.

His cremation, near Caen, was one of the nicest - and simplest - we have known. Pauline and Geoff had been passionate about music, so his life was celebrated with recorded songs. We were then invited to put a handful of rose petals on the coffin, take a moment to reflect, and then we left. In fact, Pauline eventually ended contact with these old friends and made a different life for herself, until her own death from cancer in 2019.

In July 2015 it was my own seventieth birthday. Once or twice a year, Jan and Sally and I – from *Petticoat* days - still met for lunch in London, and we often celebrated milestones. This year they bought me lunch at a restaurant in Southampton Street, just opposite where we had worked all those years ago.

I also had a tea party, with cake and candles, at home with Emma and family, and then made a cake and invited John and Linda over to celebrate again!

One extraordinary and lovely event was my visit to Paris to meet Australian playwright, Katherine Lyall Watson, the niece of my partner - author and biologist, Lyall Watson - in the mid-seventies. I had met Lyall when I was a researcher on the '*Parkinson Show'* in 1974, and we began a bizarre relationship which spanned on, but mostly off, over eighteen years.

I had first met Katherine in 1975 when, at the end of a trip to the Amazon, Lyall had taken me to meet his family at the Hwange National Park, near Victoria Falls, in Zimbabwe, then still Rhodesia. Katherine was eight years old. Thirty-three years later, on his death in 2008, I heard her do an obituary piece for 'Last Word' on Radio 4. She remembered her first meeting with her enigmatic uncle – at that family gathering – and she also mentioned me, the girlfriend!

I contacted her at the time, and we stayed loosely in touch. She was proud of her uncle and was thinking of writing a book about him. I sent her the letters I had kept and added some detail of my part in his life. I also sent her the gold necklace that Lyall's father, her grandfather, had given me when his wife had died. It felt right that Katherine should have it.

Now, aged forty-eight, she and her husband Pete were coming from their home in Brisbane to visit Paris. Maybe we could meet? Which we did - at the famous Shakespeare and Company English bookshop opposite Notre Dame. The three of us then spent the day together, which was a delight, and a memory to treasure.

In August, William and I went for a return visit to Charmouth in Dorset. We again booked a two-roomed apartment in Newlands Holiday Park, where we had stayed twelve years earlier. Charmouth, on the Jurassic coast, is a World Heritage Site, teeming with history and fossils, and the park was fifteen minutes' walk from the beach.

Unless the tide is right out and the sand appears, the beach consists of huge pebbles, and each day I grumbled that in my inadequate trainers the stones made it too difficult to walk! In the light of that, William delights in reminding me what happened next.

At the end of Lower Sea Lane, the road to the beach, is a small row of shops – including an estate agent. 'For fun' we looked in the window and were both drawn to the same house, which we asked to see. The rest is history.

From 'way back' I knew I did not like Dorset! It was somehow too 'Hardyesque' for me. Too hilly, too 'slow', too 'not me'. But William was suddenly – and unexpectedly - taken with the idea of moving. It was his choice this time, and with this house in mind, we returned home to put Priorsfield on the market. He had certainly fulfilled his two-year prediction!

In September 2015, I held a workshop in Priorsfield on *'Natural Leadership'*. It felt now that this was a fledgling group who would begin to find their own place in this emerging world, in their own way, in their own time. I could channel their directions but not necessarily 'know' them for myself. By now, and over the next few years, we were going even further into individual spiritual understanding and creativity.

It was increasingly important for each person to take their own skills forward, and in so doing find a new form of non-hierarchical leadership. The group could capture a flavour of each other's explorations and at the same time know the companionship of separate experience. This did not mean there were no psychological hiccoughs and personal anxieties to wobble the edifice; and these still needed to be expressed and addressed. But in the revelatory moments these could run alongside a bigger, more certain picture.

I now decided to revisit the novel I had written in 1990, fourteen years earlier. This was a metaphorical story, mirroring the second part of my own journey, into the 'dark feminine' and the descent into matter. In my mind this was the sister book – in novel form – to my first book *'The Wise Virgin'*. I changed the title from its original: *'Fallen Angel'* to *'Shadowplay'*.

That part of my life was long gone - since 1989 - but since the integration of spirit and matter had been the tenet of my work these last years, and as the clients and workshop participants were moving forward, I decided to look at the book 'just because'. I began a rigorous review and edit, alongside research about self-publishing.

It took a while to sell Priorsfield, and by then the house we wanted in Charmouth had been sold. So, on another visit, we found Fossils, which was then a second home and holiday let and certainly needed to be 'warmed up'. Although Charmouth is very hilly, this house offered level access to the sea – ten minutes away – and would enable William – and me - to walk freely every day. We offered on the house and were accepted. Of all places, we were going to live in Dorset!

CHAPTER THIRTEEN

October 2015: Fossils

'A place to call home?'

Yes, there were quips, that the house should be named 'Old Fossils'! But it still doesn't feel like that. Barneys Close, and the village in general, has its share of older and retired people, but not exclusively. There are also those who grew up here which makes for a kind community with many volunteers for local projects: the library, the Heritage Centre, the Food Bank, and other activities.

When we and our removal van arrived, we were heralded by the neighbours: Jane and Sharon, and Shirley opposite who produced a tray of hot sausage rolls to sustain us and the delivery men while we unloaded. We got the impression that they were pleased the house was back in the hands of permanent residents.

We are quite tightly packed in a development, though the houses are of different design, and Fossils is tucked around the corner of a T-junction. We get on really well with our opposite neighbour Chris, a building surveyor, who moved here after Shirley left. This is just as well as we are only a drive apart, and it takes neighbourhood watch to a new level!

Barneys Close - named after Barney, a Charmouth resident and renowned fossil collector in the 1960s - was developed by the farming family who own what is now the Manor Farm Leisure Centre next door. Although I do not like to be 'hemmed in' and miss the magical horizon we had in France, we are not made too aware of the summer visitors, who stay literally on the other side of our garden wall.

If I sit at my desk and look out of the window, I can see over the rooftops to the cliffs where the cows graze and the walkers climb towards Stonebarrow. At least I have that. We love the house. It suits us. And as the time goes on, I think we have settled. We now feel it would be hard to do it all again!

We surprised ourselves how quickly we set to, painting the walls in all the rooms. A nice local builder, Geoff, replaced a small window in the sitting/dining room with patio doors, which opened out the whole room. We bought spare Yorkstone slabs from Tony, our neighbour over the fence, for Geoff to make the patio and steps. He then replaced the carpet downstairs with wooden floors.

We commissioned a new kitchen, and although I was disappointed to have half the space of former sit-in kitchens, it is large enough for a small table and two chairs. The back garden had been left as a rectangular patch of field, but a local gardener agreed to dig borders, so I could make it how I wanted. I also have 'my' shed built by Tony and another friendly neighbour, Derek, for my gardening gear.

We began to get to know our environment. Whichever way we went, the area was certainly hilly, and it did curtail my love of walking. But I joined the Lyme Regis U3A monthly bird watching group and our leader Majorie was truly an expert.

We transferred our 7am café habit to Costa in Lyme Regis. Alongside a few other regulars, we would read the paper with our breakfast of choice, and an hour later enjoy an early morning walk along The Cob, before anyone else was about – apart from the joggers and cold water swimmers.

The best thing, of course, was our proximity to the beach, where we walked every day. It inspired us to learn the history of the famous Jurassic Coast and the fossil hunters, like Mary Anning of Lyme Regis. The Charmouth Heritage Centre is outstanding for this, and the prospect of fossil hunting on the beach is a magnet for tourists.

We felt proud of the three day television series '*Beach Live: The Jurassic Coast Revealed*' presented from the beach by Dan Snow in 2018 and '*David Attenborough and the Sea Dragon*', a documentary on the Ichthyosaur fossil found on the cliffs near Lyme Regis and reconstructed in the workshop of a Charmouth resident.

William joined Bridport U3A for an IT group, and it was through this branch that we found Mimi, given to us by a member who was moving away. Mimi is a vocal tabby cat with a distinctive 'Phantom of the Opera' marking down the middle of her face and, of course, we think she is beautiful. We soon learned that everyone knew Mimi because, apparently, she goes in and out of all the houses in the area, but no one has complained!

We also embarked on self-publishing '*Shadowplay*'. Jo Harrison, an IT expert who lived in France, set the text in paperback and e-book versions for Amazon's publishing platform, Create Space. I chose the cover picture from a stock photo agency and wrote cover copy, which we sent to Ryan Ashcroft, who was recommended to us by Jo. He designed the cover to Create Space specifications.

Early in October 2016 I held my first two-day workshop at Fossils, '*Beyond Soul Choice*', with Barbara, Susan, Lizzie, Brenda and Jo. The extraordinary coincidence was that Jo had left London and now lived in Lyme Regis – a mile and a half away. She had arrived sooner than us, but our choice was unrelated.

We also took a day-return train to London for fourth grandchild Ollie's eighteenth birthday. We had suggested a matinee performance of *'Funny Girl'* at the Savoy theatre, starring Sheridan Smith.

Like Lauren, Ollie was an alumnus of the Sylvia Young Stage School and was following an acting career. We attended several performances at the Barn theatre, Cirencester, one of the best producing house theatres, which proved that Ollie is certainly star material. His first role on the professional stage was in 2019 in *'Tom Brown's Schooldays'* at the Union Theatre, Southwark.

At the end of October, we took a Rail Discoveries tour to the Rhine valley in Germany. We met the tour group at St Pancras for a long and delightful journey, ending at Remagen railway station. For five days we were guided by train, funicular, boat and coach to the places of interest. We loved it all - even our table companion, who told us he was Chairman of the International Guild of Knot Tyers - for whom we raised our game and spoke animatedly about knots. His wife said very little!

'Shadowplay' was now on Amazon, but as with *'Time to Change'* we were still not good at self-marketing: I did not do social media; the main engine that gets work out. As before, the book sold mainly to my loyal constituency, and I did receive some nice reviews to put up on my website. But this comparatively small arena for my work did not stop me revisiting another book: the memoir I had begun on the kitchen table in High View, ten years earlier.

This book *'A Spot to Stand'* covered the years 1970-1995, and the 'spiritual journey' which as I say, 'is not for the fainthearted', as all my clients know.

Over these years, the journey led for me from 'knowing' (gnosis), to the ability to experience the body and its imbalances through touch sensitivity, and on to what I do now: 'channelling': an evolving ability to access a wide sweep of information. They were heady days, long gone, but as I also say: "I would not have missed the adventure for the world." We finally published the book with Create Space in 2017.

I am lucky to have my clients; the friends who understand the work I do, because I still do not speak about this side of my life to family, neighbours and some of my friends. But serendipity here in Charmouth, it emerged that Sharon, our neighbour over the other fence, was wholly sympathetic and interested.

Sharon is French Canadian from Acadia. These are descendants of the French who settled there in the 17th and 18th centuries. Married for thirty years to Tony they eventually separated but continued to live next door to each other. I gave Sharon *'Time to Change'* and then *'A Spot to Stand'*, and she discussed them with her sister in Canada. She and I would talk over the fence and have tea together; the best kind of neighbour.

Charmouth is a popular tourist area and busy in the summer, which is fine. There are organised music events like Party in the Park, and a summer market, but it is never 'heaving' like Lyme Regis. The winter is nice for being much less populated, except for the annual Christmas Day Swim, when swarms of swimmers in fancy dress, plunge into the sea at 11am on behalf of RNLI.

We had plenty of visitors ourselves. Our regular trips to Bath were now on hold - the distance in a day eventually felt too far – but Mike and Margaret came to visit locally and stayed in Lyme Regis. On one occasion, when Lizzie was with us too, we all met in a favourite restaurant The Harbour Inn.

Another place we enjoyed taking visitors like John and Barbara and Ros and Colin, was to the Tramway in Colyton.

After a return tram ride to Seaton we had the best cream tea in East Devon and Dorset.

We had little convenient space to put people up this time, so apart from Hannah, Brenda and then my Mike – who still came regularly – most of our visitors booked in at B & Bs.

On one occasion with Mike, we went to visit Thomas Hardy's birthplace and his later home Max Gate, and then met my cousin Christine and her husband John for lunch. In past years we had visited Chris and John – in Dorset – on several occasions but, somehow, had not realised how close we lived to them now! A forty minute drive along the coast, through Abbotsbury - of the famous swannery - and along the road towards Dorchester, took us to their village of West Shilvinghampton.

We were now more frequently in touch and were delighted to be included with their family in an annual lunch around Christmas. Son Roger lives in London and Ed (with Leyhan) lives in Portsmouth. Daughter Emma and her husband Andy live in Scotland.

Emma and Andy had met while working at the British Museum and Andy is now Head of Palaeobiology at National Museums, Scotland. The Jurassic Coast is a natural lure and an ideal learning ground for their young twins Ann and Katie.

I still find spending time alone refreshes my thoughts and reflections, and although William has less need to travel, my excursions give him some quiet time too! I took the opportunity to make a few two-day outings by train to places I didn't know, like The Eden Project and St Ives.

In St Ives I did an official walking tour and then visited the Barbara Hepworth museum. I had afternoon tea in the St Ives Tate. On another occasion I went to the open air Minnack

Theatre, but sadly had to leave in the middle of a matinee performance because I was roasting in the hot sunshine.

I took out a season ticket to Brucklands, a farm near Lyme Regis with a circular walk around their man-made lake which was full of water birds. We both joined the Friends of Lyme Regis museum and enjoyed U3A talks. A particular and regular favourite outing was to walk around Seaton Wetlands, taking binoculars into the hides. And I did manage, just once, to pull – and push – William up the Bridport landmark, Colmers Hill.

For a short while we joined the National Trust to visit a few stately homes in the South West: like Shute Barton and Clouds, the home of T E Lawrence. When we visited Anthony, near Plymouth, we took the opportunity to meet Fran and Derek – and Godson Michael – who were over from Spain visiting family.

We had overnight stays in Swindon to see the children, and from there we could meet Barbara and John 'half-way' for lunch in Moreton-in-the Marsh or Stow-on-the Wold. On one occasion we stayed near Newark to visit Ros and Colin in Southwell, a one-time return visit after the many times they had come to us. Then I found a new friend in Charmouth.

Charmouth is a friendly place; you tend to chat a lot when round and about, but I never expected to find a real friend. I met Lee, a jewellery designer, at the beach where we talked, and after that we kept bumping into each other. Eventually in the post office I suggested we might have coffee together and she gave me her email address.

Lee is a private person who prefers, with her husband, not to do the 'neighbourly thing', and in many ways we are unlikely friends (not least that I am twenty years older than she is). But we like each other a lot, and I feel honoured that we became early-morning beach-walking companions – and tea drinking buddies. (We have even had birthday-morning porridge on the beach!)

William is not really a group person, but at this point the idea of meeting other stroke survivors seemed a good idea, and he joined the Bridport Stroke Club. This turned out to be exactly what he needed. He found that the opportunity to sit and drink tea and talk to other stroke survivors, with a mutual acceptance and understanding of the stroke condition, was liberating.

Each week it was arranged that David Laurence, the club secretary, and his wife Heather who was a stroke survivor, would pick him up with another Charmouth member, John Davis, on their way through from Lyme Regis. (By extraordinary coincidence, it was Rev. David who married William's niece Sarah and J-P in the Forest of Dean all those years ago, but it was a while before we were reminded of that.)

As time progressed, William had begun to feel more confident of his mental and physical abilities, and about a year after he joined the club, he had the idea of writing a book about stroke. In Le Perrey he had set up a website to discuss stroke issues, but now he let this go to pursue the idea of a book.

One reason for doing this was that his first venture into disability in the 1980s was a series of videos for the Multiple Sclerosis Society. This enabled people to talk about their own situation and how MS affected them, and now he wanted to give a voice to stroke survivors in the same way. He began to select the people he would like to include.

He had access to Heather and John, who were happy to take part, and cousin Ros' husband Colin was a natural choice. Barbara and Dave – now based in Dorset - suggested their neighbour Evelyn, and Lizzie and James knew Charles in Harrogate. The Stroke Association suggested one or two more. Knowing how much he had needed my help at the time of his own strokes, he was also keen to talk to the carers as a crucial part of a stroke survivor's abilities and wellbeing.

The participants were from all walks of life and all ages. One young woman was just twenty-one, an age at which it is difficult to come to terms with reduced physicality. Her then boyfriend was unable to take the strain, but a little later we were pleased to hear that she had become engaged to someone else.

William spent several weeks travelling to record the interviews, and I offered to type them up on his return. As I went along, I added a few journalistic skills, and in 2017 we went the Create Space route again and published '*So You've Had a Stroke*'.

In April 2017, I held a two-day workshop: '*Bringing God Down to Earth*' on the influence of religion and the changing nature of God. Apart from two one-day workshops in Violet Hill Studios in St John's Wood, which the London contingency could attend easily, workshops in Fossils were becoming much looser events. I did not make official flyers but would simply email a few people who might be interested. Participants were becoming a 'core group'.

In June 2018 it was fifth grandchild Harry's 18th birthday, and on this occasion, we went back to the Watermill Theatre, Newbury for lunch, and a performance of Jez Butterworth's '*Jerusalem*'. As wild as it was, even we liked it!

Emma and James' seven children have grown up fast. They have lives of their own, but they are and always have been the nicest young people. It was daughter number two, Immy, who invited us to a surprise 50th birthday party for Emma, at the home of her boyfriend Charlie's mother.

William missed growing vegetables and the dream now was to have an allotment, with raised beds to suit his needs. He joined the Charmouth allotments waiting list, but three years on, when neighbour Tony reached the top of the list before him,

Tony offered to share his patch. He also took some space in our garden for three more raised beds and set to work.

In March 2019 we went back to Villedieu and 'the gang' were invited for a lunch at Peter and Janet's to celebrate Peter's birthday. Later that year John and Barbara came to Charmouth, and in September Jan and Barrie stayed at an Air B & B nearby, to celebrate her seventieth birthday.

We had been aware for several years that 'my' Mike was ill. He had prostate cancer and other conditions and had had bouts in hospital with septicaemia. He was stoic and inspirational in that 'I don't worry about something I can do nothing about'. And he still managed the four-hour drive from East Sussex to see us – even if now he needed a mobility scooter to be mobile. Until 2019.

In May that year, his daughter Karen rang and suggested that his condition was worsening, and if I wanted to see him, I should come now. I asked friends Monica and John, who lived close by, if they could pick me up at the station – as a favour - and take me to the house. And an hour or so later to return and take me back. Mike was now living downstairs but making the effort to talk. Di was as calm as always.

A month later I went back – with Mary – to attend his funeral, along with two hundred or so others who wished to pay their respects. He had clearly had a long and varied life with friends and acquaintances in many arenas. I miss him.

But, alongside Mike, my heart and mind were taken up by Lizzie. Over the last few years, she and James had spent three months each year in Canada. They would arrange a house swap with people in Toronto, ostensibly for James to get together with Canadian friends and make music, but they both loved it there.

James usually included a Yardbirds US tour, and Lizzie might visit a friend Anne in Florida. She had begun to take clients for channelling and Anne was a staunch supporter. Lizzie and I would be in touch through email and Skype and we could swap sessions if necessary. When she told me that she had an unexplained lump in her arm, I – and we - urged her to have it checked.

This is a story stretching over three long years. Lizzie had, as it unfolded, a rare cancer: leiomyosarcoma. She pursued alternative treatment with a Chinese herbalist, and then, on their return to France, went for a re-run of all the tests. To her, and our, horror, the consultant in Nice prescribed amputation of her arm above the elbow. This was halted at the last minute when they found a secondary lesion in the liver.

To get the best expert advice, they rented an apartment in Paris for several months, and from then on, through rounds of chemo and beyond, she and I worked with the guides almost every week. Not once did they promise a cure, but they kept steady – as I had to do – with the continuing sense – and experience - of moving through to a deeper and deeper sense of who she was.

When they came to London to consult a UK expert, James took time out to do necessary appointments, so Lizzie and I met in Kew to walk and talk and eat lovely meals nearby. When Lizzie returned to Paris and James needed to stay in London, it was Barbara who stepped in, travelling to Paris in the unbearable thirty-four degree heat. During that time, James came down to see us for two days, staying at a nearby B & B, needing, I'm sure, a little TLC.

At the end of October 2019, Barbara and Susan came to Charmouth and we did some work together, which Susan described later as "being given all manner of tools to help us step into the new". We were profoundly aware of Lizzie and sad that she could not be with us this time.

In January 2020, when James had a long term commitment for a US Yardbird tour, I took the train to Draguignan, via an overnight stay in Paris, and was picked up by their friend Vanya. She drove me to Bargemon to spend several days with Lizzie.

Her hair had regrown into a little bubble of curls, but by this time, there was nothing further that medicine could do. She had refused more chemo, and complementary medicine, her only option now, meant she was taking many pills. She had tried and would continue to try everything.

We had a lovely time. We could walk – slowly - and talk – gently - and eat food prepared by me to the best of my ability. We would sit round her open fire and go to bed early. When Lizzie needed to rest, I explored the village, which was so like Le Castellet, my own walled Medieval village when I lived in the Var. When I left, Susan came from Guernsey (she and Ian had now left Switzerland) and stayed for two weeks while Lizzie and I kept working with guidance.

In January 2020, on that trip to France, there was nothing in the air about *Coronavirus*, but two months later it was here and there and everywhere. In early May the year before, I had held a workshop in Charmouth: '*Realigning to 2020*', with Susan, Barbara, Mary, Jo and also Victoria, who might normally have attended a London workshop.

It had been suggested that the real 2012 - prophesied as a momentous time of change - was in fact 2017. And, furthermore, that the effects of this turning point moment would be felt in 2020.

We could never have envisaged how true that was. In that workshop the guides had given the participants a sense of their own individual realignment to a positive future. If we ever needed to hold on to that experience it was now.

CHAPTER FOURTEEN

2020

A master light lies the length of the valley,
Its mountainous presence deeply felt.
Reciprocal communion existing in the vast,
Eternal possibility that is being and relating:
An echo of precision and beauty that is its peace

In this reflecting light,
Here I Am! Wholly me!
Not on my knees
But standing free,
Softly…to walk on, in all my glory,
into the kindness of the evening's golden glow.
Elisabeth McCrae McCarty 2019

Lizzie died in June 2020 at the age of fifty-eight. I do not know why she had to die. She was the epitome, had reached the pinnacle, of all I had wanted to teach over the last twenty-five years – and more. Perhaps that is why. During the last years, and especially over the last months and weeks of her life, she experienced with the guides – mine and her own - realms and dimensions through her body and through nature beyond anything I could ever imagine.

Perhaps Lizzie was just too soon. She needed the journey; she needed the release from personal and collective history while the planet was still 'dense' enough for the astral plane to operate. Many years earlier the guides had suggested that soon this 'emotional' plane would lift off, and those who came back to planet Earth would be beyond that.

Earth would no longer be a planet of love and healing, over-lighted by the Moon, but a planet of beauty and truth, aligned to Venus. Lizzie had found that place, *was* that place. She was beauty. Perhaps she can come back soon.

When she went into a coma, James held the phone to her ear, and I could still speak to her. The guides gave her a message which James read to her daily, knowing she could hear, and a friend read it again at her funeral, which of course we could not attend, due to *Covid-19*.

Covid has shaken the world to its core. *Covid* has shown up inequalities, and with the last US Administration highlighting hate and division, it has been a time to blow off steam, for the rage of humanity to rise up out into the atmosphere, a global warming that has made us anxious and fearful.

But the world has turned, say the guides. We can return to a cooler humanity. There are opportunities for each individual to become newly calibrated without the legacy of the past difficulties and woundedness, insecurity and fear that have dogged us all throughout our incarnations. So much so that we will almost forget how difficult the past has been.

The underlying issue for humanity, say the guides, has been narcissism or at least self-centredness. Because we have all been wounded over lifetimes of experience on planet Earth, we have all, to a greater or lesser extent, needed to feel special, buoyed up, recognised and admired - writ so very large in the nature of Donald Trump.

In need of such reassurance, we think of ourselves first, but when we strive and compete to be seen, there is a natural inequality, waste and greed. I feel the work I have done in the last twenty-five years has been to give people the experience that the guilts, shames, worries and fears that have come from way back in their incarnational history and bled through into this life, can be seen for what they are, moved through, and then let go.

When you truly love who you are, and know that loving yourself is enough, the world changes. When you know you are important to yourself, when you are in love with yourself, you think of others, and find greater contentment in life. I have seen the stretched, fearful, damaged heart mend in an extraordinary manner, so we can sit comfortably in our conscious bodies, and realise that the engine of life is loving kindness.

Since my mid-twenties, I have believed – known - there is to be a new movement, a new day, a new dawn, the possibility of a different relationship to life. I have seen fully grounded people live 'without edges', opening up channels to new sources, new dimensions, new creativity. It is important to know that it is ordinary to be extraordinary. It needs no accolades; it just is.

For me Lizzie's death, has marked a completion of this last twenty-five year era, when the focus has been towards working with clients and teaching. For me, and all of us, this is the moment of change.

The workshops over the last years have taken participants beyond 'the journey', beyond time, to soul choice and the New Story. Alice Bailey was a writer of more than twenty-four books on theosophical subjects and was first to coin the term New Age.

The majority of her work she described as being telepathically dictated by a Master of Wisdom, 'The Tibetan', or DK – Djwal Khul. In other words, she was channelling. She died in 1949.

She wrote of an Age of Aquarius, where there would be a unified society, including a global spirit of religion, and she wrote an exposition of the Seven Rays of Life, which are presented as the fundamental energies behind, and exist throughout, all manifestation. We, humanity, would soon be leaving the sixth ray and entering the seventh.

The sixth ray 'Devotion to God', under the Master Jesus, describes the last thousands of years, when in the early days of religion, man gave an all-knowing, all-seeing God all the power to understand the wisdom of consciousness.

As we enter the seventh ray, 'the Wisdom of God' (under the Master Djwal Khul), we can begin to understand the nature of our own God-Self, to realise that consciousness is the never-ending story, in order to understand the nature of Life Itself.

This is not quite my language and Alice Bailey was not my pursuit, but I could say that all the workshops over these twenty-five years have been an exploration of this understanding.

Lorna Bevan has a different language; that of astrology, but she echoes the same: an era of change. "The New Year 2021 began on December 21st 2020 at the Capricorn Solstice under the rare celestial conjunction of Saturn/Jupiter at 0 degrees Aquarius. And it marks far, far more than a new year. It is initiating an entirely new era of humanity.

It is not going to change overnight, but we can begin to stop looking outside and focus on our own originality.

As Lorna says, so eloquently, "Personal neutrality is only accessible from this Diamond Space within – not indifference, not spiritual by-passing, not escapism, but the ability to dance with the waves of evolutionary change."

I will continue to channel the Masters of Wisdom, which for me is about linking to my own far reaches and multi-dimensionality, although it may come in a different guise now.

I began the last twenty-five years by saying I did not want to save the world, but only to save you and me. I have worked with dozens and dozens of fabulous people, who have saved themselves and are ready to step up to the plate. There are many now who, in so many different ways, can selflessly put their heart and mind and spirit into living their truth in the clearest, kindest and most conscious way, and by doing so play their part in making the world a better place.

I'll just wait and see. What I do know is that deep down inside me - wholly embodied – is a stream of life, that is Life Itself, and holds 'all that is'. It is different; it is real, and it just is: A Place to Call Home.

Charmouth, January 2021

AND SO

"Three things in human life are important.
The first is to be kind.
The second is to be kind.
And the third is to be kind"

Henry James

From the Masters of Wisdom:
"The moment of change will bring such extraordinary recognitions, wisdom and understanding, that humanity has passed the ring-pass-not between the rigidity of the earth and the pliability of the universe.

In many ways earth's rigidity has been a learning school; for the waking of humanity to its incredible heritage; that of being a multi-dimensional, spiritual being, rather than the rigid, materialistic as it seems to be today.

The learning school has been absolutely vital in this recognition. It has been a journey for souls to reach a level of consciousness whereby at one level they return to spirit and multi-dimensional reality, but also, they attain it. They re-enter it. They re-member it in a new way in an evolutionary way. So that spiritualised beings can understand in consciousness that this is who they truly are.

Humanity has had to learn, to integrate its entire history: from entering earth's rigid atmosphere as molecules of experience, through the whole evolutionary cycle to become realised beings. This has meant they have had to remember themselves from that original molecule, through to this current, material world which has created huge stresses and strains – and on to a bigger, wider picture of connectedness, within the emergent humanity.

The most important thing for us right now is to know and recognise that all humanity is spiritual in origin. Therefore, all humanity is equal in the eyes of universal understanding. Throughout its history, humanity has been unable to perceive equality. Until now, life has been about fight and flight, about dominance and servility. About reaching for the stars no matter who you tread on along the way.

But over these last years, more and more people have recognised that there is more to their inner world than this mighty, greedy, trampling attitude that has evolved to its zenith. Slowly but surely, they have understood, worked hard, and moved through the history mankind has created - life after life, death after death.

They have reached the knowledge that life itself can be spiritualised, and that if you treat your life gently with intention, with respect, then you can treat others gently with respect. Life Itself, on earth, is where life can be lived within a spiritualised worldview.

In many ways, this journey can be defined by the solar system. Astrology has given man a map of his journeying, his experience of a material world view. It is by experiencing all these transiting energies that he has traversed to the limits of the life of humanity in the rigid, material world of earth; completed the hero's journey.

But the breakthrough has been made. Our experience has gone beyond the solar system, into our multi-dimensional universe of understanding, the beauty, wisdom and truth that all beings are equal.

It is as simple as that. All beings are equal."

Printed in Great Britain
by Amazon